INTERMITTENT ~~FASTING~~ BLASTING

THE SIMPLE TRUTH BEHIND CONSISTENTLY LOSING WEIGHT AND KEEPING IT OFF...
FOR GOOD!

WILLIAM KING
FOREWORD BY DR. MAURICE WERNESS

This book on Intermittent Blasting is written for anyone interested in getting the maximum benefit for their health and weight loss. Many scientific studies and articles have been cited confirming the various health benefits mentioned in this book and are culled from reliable research available online. Where possible, these websites are listed in the following format should the reader desire further research or clarification:

> ▣ http://www.cdc.gov/healthyyouth/obesity/facts.htm

I have done my best to categorize these links for further study so that the reader can dig deeper as they so desire, both in the text and in the Appendix at the end of this book. I encourage the reader to pursue their own research in regards to intermittent fasting, superfoods and the many health benefits these ideas provide. All sites were verified as operational at the time of printing.

Visit us online at IntermittentBlasting.com

ACKNOWLEDGMENTS

I would like to thank my wife Annette and my son Liam for their constant support and allowing me brief periods of solitude so I could conceptualize, write, and complete this book.

I would like to thank David Iversen for his tireless additions, deletions, re-writing, re-editing, re-formatting, and continuously putting up with the curve balls I've hurled his way throughout the writing of this book. David was very instrumental in every aspect of developing Intermittent Blasting and this book would not be nearly as interesting without his ability as a wordsmith and many, many edits and re-writes.

Thank you Ti Bergenn for your meticulous eye in helping edit the grammar and punctuation in this book. Thank you, Juliana Norris, Chris Duke, and Stephanie Nesbitt for your valuable input and a very special thank you to my dear friend Louan Gideon who provided valuable feedback before succumbing to cancer after a valiant struggle.

I would also like to thank Scott Carr, Sam Carver, and John Huffstetler for their friendship and constant constructive critiquing. Thanks to Amy Greene, Pat Howlett, Terry and Carole Sheffield, Maggie Scofield, Chase Jordan, Sally Bowman, Ed Hackim and Tommy Lewis, for being among the first to try Intermittent Blasting; not to mention acting as guinea pigs for my many experiments and concoctions over the years. Thank you, Marie Smith-Krebs and Bud Curtis for kick-starting my journey of fasting and cleansing and providing support in subsequent years.

Thank you, Ryan Ray, Kimberly Winborne, Bishop Wymond Burton, Beverly Hester, Wanda Thomas, David Ray, Alfonso Garcia, Dr. Puja Wentworth, Christian Welte, Bruce Henderson, Janis

Pulliam and Derek and Malika Becton for your many contributions and sharing Intermittent Blasting with others. With your efforts, we have now helped people lose (literally) tons of pounds of unwanted and unhealthy fat.

Special thanks to Sally Beare for her expertise into Longevity Hot Spots and her feedback and assistance in writing this book. Also special thank you goes to my personal physician and fellow warrior in the good fight against sickness and disease, Dr. Maurice Werness, for his constant support and kind, thoughtful words in the forward of this book.

FOREWORD

William King walked into my clinic as a tall, upright, slender man. The most prominent thing I remember about him was his dogged determination to figure out what was going on with his body. He held firmly to the belief that disease was not some random accident. He believed if he could understand what was going on with his body, he could support the body in such a way, that it would self-correct.

This was a rare belief system twenty years ago, when I first met him. Today it still flies in the face of conventional wisdom. It is the determination of individuals like William King and their belief in the truth of an idea, no matter what conventional wisdom says, that ultimately changes the world.

If I've learned one thing in my twenty years as a Naturopathic physician, it's that you can't trick Mother Nature. We are a part of nature. Life functions with the laws of nature. There is an intrinsic intelligence to life. If one tries to bend or break laws of nature the organism always responds with a primary or secondary reaction that is often contrary to the intended goal. A good example of this is the growing problem of antibiotic resistant "superbugs" due to the overuse of antibiotics. Knowing this, I believe it is best to try to understand the laws of nature and work with them not against them.

When it comes to weight management the common notion is that if we just limit the calories consumed and increase the energy burned through exercise, then we are going to lose weight. But this notion does not take into account the intrinsic intelligence of the body. When you limit the calories consumed by the body for an extended period of time, the body thinks it's starving. Since the main job of life is to survive, the body thinks it's starving when it doesn't get enough calories, and it is going to do everything it can to lower its metabolic

5

rate so it can survive as long as possible. And that is just what it does. As a matter of fact, studies have shown that with extended dieting the metabolic rate can stay in a depressed state for up to a year after the dieting ends.

During the early stages of human beings on the planet, food was not as readily available as it is now. Human beings would often go days between meals. During these periods of fasting the body would shift into a period of cleansing and rejuvenation. Now that food is readily available, the body rarely has an opportunity to shift into the cleansing and rejuvenation mode, which is the best opportunity to burn fat. Fat burning begins after an individual has used up the energy from his or her last meal, which can take as long as 8 to 10 hours.

Intermittent Blasting is based on how the body was designed to function optimally. Intermittent Blasting is a natural form of weight management based on the body's own intrinsic intelligence. As people develop the healthy habit of Intermittent Blasting, they often tell us that their body begins to crave this time of rest and rejuvenation. Nature is the most powerful force in the physical world. Therefore, it is always better to work with nature rather than against it. Intermittent Blasting works in perfect alignment with the way our bodies were designed to function.

This wonderful book explains the details and some of the science behind why Intermittent Blasting is a revolution in health and healthy weight loss. Read it and learn the secret to healthy weight management and enjoy the path of creating health and longer life, full of high quality moments.

Doctor Maurice Werness, Naturopathic Physician

TABLE OF CONTENTS

PART I: DISCOVERING HEALTH

Chapter 1: My Personal Journey to Health

There is an undeniable truth in our society today. Even as we make advancements in modern medicine, our health is getting steadily worse as incidents of heart disease, diabetes and cancer increase. Obesity is at epidemic proportions and worsening. At the same time, we are suffering from symptoms of malnourishment even as we get fatter and fatter! Most who lose weight on a traditional diet end up gaining the weight back and often, in the long run, gain even more weight than they lost.

Two events in my life put this dichotomy into stark relief and suggest a potential solution to our problems. Intermittent Blasting is the next logical step in my personal health journey and one I can't wait to share.

A Defining Childhood Event

From an early age, I have been interested in how what we eat can affect how healthy we are. When I was a very small boy growing up in central North Carolina I spent many summers on my grandfather's farm. My cousins and I would gather to play hide-and-seek in the cornfields, pick grapes and ride ponies - everything you can imagine happening on a family farm. My grandfather was a strong man, hoisting us up on his back while we laughed and giggled, pretending to be airplanes or race cars.

One day my mother called me into the living room and told me that my grandfather needed to have his leg amputated due to his diabetes. I had never heard the word "amputation" before and when my mother explained it to me it freaked me out. She told me my grandfather's diabetes was destroying his leg and the best solution

11

was to cut it off. This did not compute in my young mind. I saw him take shots for his diabetes but he never really seemed sick. This brought it all home. How had he gotten this illness? Did a snake bite him? Were there evil elves in the woods that put a curse on him? Was he being punished by God or cursed by Satan? How could my robust active grandfather have to have one of his legs taken away?

"Diabetes," my mother explained, "is a disease you get when you don't eat right. But don't worry...your grandfather will be fine in no time."

How could this be? You eat food and it makes you sick? I thought food made you strong...eating keeps you alive. How on earth could eating make anyone sick? And is there something we can do to prevent this from happening, I wondered.

In a few weeks my grandfather was up and about on his new prosthetic leg. He was a bit slower and more awkward with his steps, but he was the same old grandfather, and we continued to enjoy our time together especially in the warm summer months.

A couple of years later my mom came to me again and said my grandfather had to have his other leg removed for the same reason: diabetes - caused by what he ate. This time it didn't really concern me because when it happened before, he quickly returned to his old self again.

Yet this time turned out to be completely different. This was more than forty years ago. Today you see Olympic runners gliding around the track on two prosthetic legs. But forty years ago, prosthetics were wooden and very cumbersome. My grandfather could manage with one prosthetic leg but two confined him to a wheelchair and he turned into a completely different person overnight. He had always been active and happy, always laughing and making others laugh, but now he just sat in his wheelchair and stared out into the distance never saying anything to anyone. In fact, I can't remember him ever saying another word to me.

From that moment on, my mind made a clear connection between what we eat and how we feel and live. Now, I don't claim I ran right out as a kid and became a vegetarian or anything like that. But the connection between eating and health had been made. In the meantime, life went on...

Teenage Years

In my late teens and twenties, I was a typical kid growing up in the New South suburbia of Raleigh, North Carolina. I learned to play the drums and soon hooked up with some friends and formed a band. We called ourselves "Destiny" and we were pretty good. I resolved to make the drums my life.

William King (far left) with Destiny in the early 1980s

We played clubs throughout North and South Carolina, traveling by van or car from gig to gig. It was pretty much what you'd expect - loud rock and roll music- partying and having a good time. I loved performing and I always enjoyed experiencing the reaction of the crowd. My life's goal from a young age was to become a professional musician. I had made many contacts in the music industry and people liked my ability and my enthusiasm and I wanted to go further.

At the same time, I was active in other areas of my life and had discovered snow skiing and felt a similar thrill gliding down a mountain as I did performing live in front of hundreds or thousands of people. I loved to find time to get out and ski as much as I could. I was happy with my music, my life and my newfound hobby.

Tragic Accident

Then one day, I suffered a tragic accident on the slopes. I failed to navigate an icy turn and went flying off the course. I'm a bit fuzzy on the details even now, but I found myself lying in the frigid snow for nearly an hour in zero-temperature weather, with a wind chill of forty below, before the rescue personnel arrived. I was in an enormous amount of pain and I couldn't move from the waist down. Eventually I was airlifted off the mountain to a local hospital where I discovered I had a broken ischium, which is part of the pelvis.

Fortunately, after many months of extensive rehab I began to learn to walk again. I started with crutches, graduated to a cane and after a year or so, I could walk unassisted. But even after I could walk again I still suffered with a great deal of pain. I could no longer play the drums. My career as a professional musician was over.

My doctors initially prescribed a variety of anti-inflammatory medications and steroids. Eventually I was taking mind-altering drugs to help manage the pain. Each medication had a variety of unwanted side effects that could only be managed with the use of more medications. Soon, I found myself taking a cocktail of pharmaceuticals on a daily basis.

I can't determine with certainty which medication caused my health to deteriorate or if it was a combination of all the medications, but over a period of a few years I suddenly found myself living with a laundry list of chronic ailments. It was a gradual process that began with me noticing that late in the day my eyes were bloodshot and dry. And at first it was no big deal. Then I noticed that I would get sick more frequently. I also started sleeping longer. My usual eight hours of sleep a night turned into thirteen. I became more irritable and began to have bouts of depression. I gained more than thirty pounds, and no matter what I tried to do I couldn't seem to lose the extra weight. I had been in good shape my entire life and now friends were saying I was portly. Day by day my health worsened dramatically.

Chronic Disease

I remember during this time being introduced to the concept of "chronic disease." I would go for a visit with an optometrist and he would say I had "chronic dry eyes." I would visit the dermatologist and he would say I had "chronic dry skin." I would go to the neurologist for a constant headache and he would say I had "chronic migraines." I quickly learned that "chronic" meant that this was something that I would have to live with for the rest of my life. I could not understand how taking a handful of pills every day that were supposed to help me could have caused this much damage.

I live about thirty minutes from Durham, N.C., which is known as "The City of Medicine," so I was seeing some of the very best "specialists" and the answer was always the same. Take another pharmaceutical drug and learn to "manage" this condition for the rest of your life. I once had a shot of Novocain under my left eye so the doctor could cauterize one of my tear ducts shut with the hope of my eyes retaining more moisture. I went to doctor after doctor and my symptoms continued to worsen.

Eventually I hit rock bottom. I had always been in great health and now I had chronic dry eyes, chronic dry skin, chronic fatigue syndrome, tinnitus and depression. I was overweight by thirty pounds, I was sleeping thirteen hours a day, I was sick constantly. I was continually on antibiotics because I was unable to get well. I eventually gave up all hope of ever feeling better.

Then I realized: It wasn't me I should be giving up on. It was the methods of "treatment" that seemed to be the root cause of all these

15

problems. So instead I gave up on the method of treatment and in so doing, found a whole new life; a life of hope and optimism with a totally different paradigm of wellness. I abandoned the concept of suppressing symptoms with pharmaceuticals and replaced it with the concept of addressing the underlying cause.

I learned that our human body is designed to self-correct; to heal itself. But the only way to get from where I was to where I wanted to be was to take drastic measures. So, one day I took a leap of faith that took every ounce of courage I could muster.

A New Life

There's a story I like to think of from time to time. There's an old hound dog lying on the front porch and he's whining in pain. A friend stops by and asks the dog's owner, "What's wrong with your dog?"

The owner replies, "He's lying on a nail." The friend says, "Why doesn't he just move?"

The owner says, "He's not in enough pain."

That's how we all feel sometimes, isn't it? We can tolerate a little pain and over time we can even become used to it, until we don't remember what life without pain was like. We get used to life lying on the nail and forget that all we have to do is move.

One day I decided I was in enough pain and had to get off that nail. I needed to do something drastic. Totally drastic. The first thing I decided to do was to go off all my medications. 100 percent pharmaceutical-free, not even an aspirin. "Cold turkey" they call it. I had been taking a cocktail of medications for so long, my body and mind were relying on them, expecting them to be there. Then one day they weren't there. I woke up one day and said, "It's either the meds...or me." And I have never taken them again.

16

As helpful as it turned out for me eventually, this is something I do not recommend. It was excruciatingly painful to go through at the time. In hindsight, I would have weaned off the meds over time, but I made my choice and it was literally "do or die."

Discovering the Power of Fasting

For several days, I was as sick as I have ever been. At times, I thought I was going to die. I began to pour through books on nutrition and health, reading everything I could get my hands on. One day, a life-long friend introduced me to the concept of fasting and cleansing to improve health. He told me about a clinic that was scheduled to be in town and this "cleanse" was supposed to "cure anything". That turned out to be a bit of an exaggeration but I could tell my friend was excited about it, so I decided to check it out.

Through my research, I learned that a variety of lifestyle and environmental factors had overwhelmed my body with toxicity. I became convinced that this toxicity was at the root of my health problems. This cleansing clinic promised to rid the body of toxins so I decided to make a commitment. The clinic consisted of a seven-day juice fast and colon cleanse with classes on nutrition and fasting for several hours each day.

To be honest, at the time the things I learned over the course of that week seemed totally crazy. I thought the instructors were completely out of their minds. Remember, I was from the South and grew up on a typical southern diet. The instructors taught us there was a connection between the digestive tract and the brain and that it is important to eat an organic plant-based diet. They spoke about how things like juicing can greatly improve your health. Today many of these principles have been confirmed both anecdotally and with modern science as you will see in the annotations and references in this book. But twenty years ago, it just seemed like madness to most people but eventually the techniques began to click for me.

Over the period of seven days I drank six drinks a day that contained organic, raw apple juice and a mixture of herbs and ingredients designed to cleanse the bodily organs like the liver, gallbladder, lymphatic system and colon. I had no idea how eating differently, fasting and cleansing would help my eyes, skin, energy level, weight management, pain, immune system and more, but remember, my life was miserable and Western medicine was out of options. Desperation is a great motivator.

Now, it didn't happen overnight...but over time I began to see improvement. The first positive indication was when my eyes and skin began to feel slightly moister. I was still fuzzy on the connection between what I ate and how my eyes and skin felt, but I knew what was happening had to be a good indication that something was finally moving in the right direction.

One of the key lessons I learned during that time was that the human body is in one of two states at all times. We are either digesting or restoring (the process of detoxing and cleansing our cells). The body does not do both at once. I learned that when the body is finished digesting, it enters a phase called autophagy. Autophagy is a self-cleaning mechanism the body uses for restoration. But autophagy can only begin after digestion is fully complete. The 2016 Nobel Prize was won by Yoshinori Ohsumi and based on his research into autophagy, which will also be explained in detail later in this book. To promote this state of restoration, we were encouraged to delay our first meal of the day as late as possible and then have fresh juice or a smoothie so we could quickly get back to the process of self-cleaning. The instructor didn't refer to either of these techniques as "intermittent fasting" but that's exactly what they were. Today, I realize that these concepts assisted our ancestors with their health and weight management and they can also form the basis of a healthy life for us in the modern world.

Retaking Control of My Life

Eventually, more of my "chronic" symptoms began to fade or disappear entirely. I redoubled my regimen, constantly improving my diet, and fasting regularly to cleanse my system. I tried so many different regimens I eventually became adept at fasting and cleansing.

Today my health has been fully restored. Over a period of time when most people expect their health to begin to deteriorate, I've experienced just the opposite. Today my body fat is between 10 percent and 12 percent and my blood pressure and blood-sugar levels are exceptional. In my 20's I consistently recorded cholesterol levels in the range of 250 and my doctor told me that I had inherited high cholesterol from my parents. High cholesterol was "genetic" he said. Today my cholesterol is under 200 and even got down to 130 for a time, strictly from my diet. I do not take any medications whatsoever, not so much as an aspirin.

Over the years I've experienced more than one hundred cleansing regimens that include juice or water fasting for a duration ranging from one day to three weeks, with the majority being around seven days. Now I fast or Blast (I will explain later in the book) one or two days per week quite frequently and up to seven days occasionally. It's something I have come to firmly believe in and something I feel is necessary for anyone who wishes to return to, or achieve optimal health.

Fasting to improve health is well established for most of recorded history; in fact, Hippocrates, Socrates, and Plato all recommended fasting for health recovery. Religious fasts are common in both Western and Eastern spiritual thought. Benjamin Franklin said, "The best of all medicines is resting and fasting." Mark Twain remarked, "A little starvation can really do more for the average sick man than can the best medicines and the best doctors."

Today fasting and cleansing regimens are gaining mainstream acceptance. Even some Western- trained medical doctors are embracing detoxification regimens as a means of restoring health and well-being to their patients. I believe we will be healthier as a result. One of the primary principles behind Intermittent Blasting is something I know for sure from personal experience: Given proper nutrition and rest, the body will heal itself.

In the next chapters I will identify the root causes of our ill-health epidemic. To understand how to fix a problem, you must first understand how that problem came about. There are two great crises facing us in modern society - obesity and malnourishment. While these two seem to be polar opposites, I will show how they are actually tied together in a Catch 22-type paradox only our modern society could create.

Then we will discuss a new regimen that combines the benefits of a super-nutrient blast with fasting to achieve the best possible results for your body's health and weight management. This is Intermittent Blasting and you will be amazed with the results. You will lose weight, have more energy, increase mental clarity, and sleep soundly through the night. Who knows? Maybe you too will wean yourself off some of those medications your doctors said you had to take for the rest of your life.

Chapter 2: A Brand New Approach

The "Diet" Trap

For far too long our society has been obsessed with unhealthy methods of weight loss: fad diets, all sorts of "snake oil" and mystery chemicals we ingest to find a way to lose the weight our doctors tell us is so critical to lose to experience a healthy life. And the doctors are right. Despite decades of diet fads, more than two-thirds of

Americans are overweight (68 percent) and more than one-third are obese (34 percent). Overall, the percentage of adults over the age of twenty who are considered obese is up from 22 percent in 1994 to 34 percent in 2008, and rising.

There is solid scientific evidence that explains why dieting does not work for us. When we can find a diet that does work, the overwhelming majority of us just end up gaining back all the weight we lost...and then some. Or even worse, we end up malnourished and with a slower metabolism than we had before we went on the diet. Our bodies are simply not designed to lose weight in the manner that traditional diets recommend.

A New Approach to Fasting

I travel quite a bit for business and while traveling around the U.S. several years ago I noticed a trend. When I travel, it's very difficult for me to find fresh organic food, which accounts for the majority of what I eat, so invariably I find myself at a juice bar of some sort. I began to noticed in major cities like New York, San Francisco, Los Angeles, Miami, and Detroit, there are companies popping up that offer organic, cold-pressed juice and juice cleanses. I've been juicing and incorporating various forms of juice cleansing into my life for over two decades. But I had never seen these types of products offered on the market, available to consumers in a turn-key fashion. I noticed when visiting these juice companies, all of them seemed to be doing a swift business, and they all seemed to be quickly accumulating a lot of "Likes" on their Facebook pages, which led me to believe they are doing quite well. This caught my attention because the majority of cleanses I had done have been quite arduous. Why would something so taxing and dreadful become so popular? I wondered.

As it turns out, most of these cleanses aren't nearly as difficult as the ones I had done and they can even be somewhat fun and

21

enjoyable. The juices recommended for the majority of these cleanses are delicious! This is in stark contrast to most of the cleanses I had used over the years. And most of these cleanses are properly designed so that you receive enough balanced nutrition to kept you well-satisfied throughout the day.

A few years ago, I started a wellness company based on the lives of people living in what are termed "Longevity Hot Spots." We developed a nutritional supplement based on the diets of the people that lived there. This product incorporated fermented "superfoods" (nutritionally dense foods sourced organically), probiotics, minerals and enzymes.

I decided to develop a cleansing regimen that involved this fermented, nutrient-dense product mixed with fresh vegetable and fruit juices. I used a variety of juices and only the very best ingredients. I shared the concept of this cleanse with three friends: Pat, Amy and Juliana. Pat loved the idea. As it happens, he had put on some weight he wanted to lose and he had recently read about intermittent fasting as a solution. I told him my regimen was also a form of intermittent fasting. Instead of lower amounts of nutrition, I wanted to find a way to "blast" the body with high amounts of quality, nutrient dense nutrition. We had a great conversation about it and he seemed genuinely interested in trying it. I shared it with Juliana who owns a med spa and she was very receptive as well.

Then one day, I was sitting in my office when my co-worker Amy started talking to me about cleanses and detoxifying, as she knew my history of experience in this area. I suggested that she try my new regimen I had given to Pat and Juliana. I explained that her body was either in digesting mode or cleansing mode but never both at once and this would allow her body time to rest and rejuvenate. I told her she would probably feel just fine with one caveat; considering her daily caffeine intake, I suggested she consume a little caffeine (from black coffee or green tea) each day. I explained how a sudden withdrawal from caffeine would likely cause a bad headache and ruin her experience and dampen her enthusiasm.

She did a three-day cleanse, taking five servings of our product as I suggested, and she lost five pounds. Much to her surprise, she was alert and focused the entire time and slept like a baby at night.

I didn't realize this at the time, but there were other people in the office listening in on our conversation. In no time, there were three or four people in our office who were doing this introductory three-day program. Then I started hearing of other people who were doing it. Husbands of the women and wives of the men in the office were trying it too!

"Just what's going on?" I asked myself. Suddenly there were eight or ten people, who, totally by their own accord, were choosing to abstain from solid food for three straight days without prodding or encouragement of any kind and everyone was having great results. Suddenly people were posting pictures of the readings from their bathroom scales on Facebook. I found that some people were doing it for the second and third time. Excitement was building. It was fun hearing everyone share their experiences. Alfonzo, one of my friends, gathered six of his friends together and collectively they lost forty-two pounds in just three days. Everyone felt good, although the first day was a bit challenging for most, but they were going about their daily activities as usual, while feeling good...and losing weight.

On average, people lost four to eight pounds in just three days! For someone who struggles with their weight, it's amazing to hear that you can lose four to eight pounds in just three days, but with this method, it's almost impossible not to do just that.

Not only were people losing weight, they were feeling great and getting healthy. Their blood pressure, blood sugar, and cholesterol levels were going down quickly which are more signs of healthy weight loss. Also, people began to realize just how many unnecessary calories they take in on a daily basis, how much junk food they consume, and how habitual food is in their lives. People also noticed a clearing of the mind and of the eyes and skin due to the cleansing aspects. So, the positive effects are much greater than just the weight loss. Someone said something about how it doesn't feel like a fast, but a "blast." They blast their cells with nutrition and they are having a blast losing weight. It occurred to me that "blast" was a good shorthand to reference this new method of weight loss and Intermittent Blasting was born.

Chapter 3: Superfoods Make Intermittent Fasting a Blast!

At this point, we had created an entirely new concept. While the benefits of traditional fasting have been known for ages, as we will discuss later in this book, it is not something that our modern lifestyles easily support. It can be a long and sometimes arduous process. This is why most people cringe when you mention that you are fasting (or at best look at you with a sense of wonder as if you possessed some kind of super-human quality that they lack.)

Intermittent fasting, however, is something that can be easily achieved by most, if not all, people in today's society. But can it be as effective as a traditional fast? Recently, intermittent fasting is showing great promise in clinical trials with both humans and laboratory animals. As we detail later in the Chapter 11, numerous studies have confirmed that intermittent fasting holds just as much benefits and promise as traditional long-term fasting.

Two Fundamental Types of Intermittent Fasting

First, let's talk about the two basic types of intermittent fasting: *time restricted feeding* and *periodic fasting*. Both methods allow the body to rest the digestive tract so it can perform the necessary restorative and repair work lacking in our fast-paced modern world.

Time restricted feeding simply decreases the window of time in which you eat each day. Remember before, when I mentioned that my fasting instructor said to delay the first meal of the day and then to have only juice or a smoothie to break the fast? She was basically instructing me to only consume solid foods from around noon (lunch time) until around six p.m. each day. This allows the digestive tract approximately 12-14 hours a day to rest and recuperate before having to tackle the task of digestion again.

The popular diet entitled *The 8 Hour Diet* requires participants to eat only during an eight-hour window of time each day, leaving sixteen hours for the body to do its restorative work and fat burning. Fresh juice or a smoothie is much easier on the digestive process and will allow your body to get back to the task of cleansing much faster than a breakfast of proteins and fats. Proteins can take more than four to six hours to digest while most carbohydrate foods are digested in three hours or less, some in as little as twenty minutes.

Periodic fasting typically calls for the participant to consume approximately 25% of their usual daily calorie intake during a period of hours or days. The U.S. Department of Agriculture daily calorie recommendations for men and women depending on a variety of variables such as size and activity level are:

- Men: 2000-3000
- Women: 1600-2400

Using this range of 1600-3000 calories per day, 25% would be 400-750 calories per day.

Examples of this intermittent fasting technique are the *5/2 Diet* where you eat normally five days a week and greatly reduce your calories two days a week. *The Every Other Day Diet* also known as

"Alternate Day Fasting" is where participants reduce calories on alternating days.

Give the Body Time to Rest, Rejuvenate and Burn Fat

Both of these intermittent fasting techniques have one thing in common: they allow the body time off from the digestive process so it can focus on rest, rejuvenation and healing. One of the first principles I was taught when I began to change my health was that the body is always either *digesting* or *restoring* but it never does both at the same time. You want to give the body as much time as possible each day to rest and rejuvenate.

There are really two principles at play here and they each serve different purposes. Giving your body long periods of not having to digest food will greatly enhance the restoration and detoxification process. But it will also help you burn fat more efficiently. This is because it takes around six to eight hours for the body to metabolize its stored glycogen; after that you shift to fat burning for energy. If you eat every eight hours or so you are constantly replenishing your glycogen stores making it far more difficult for your body to use your fat stores as fuel. Giving your body 12 to 14 hours or more between meals will kick in the fat-burning mechanisms and make it easier and quicker to lose weight.

Building A Better Fast

The conundrum is this: we are healthiest when we fast intermittently because that is the way our bodies are designed. But the same design makes us hungry all the time and we crave food to store away as fat for the lean times that never come. The result is epidemic obesity that causes health problems our ancestors could never have imagined in their world.

As important as rest and rejuvenation is to our bodies neither time restricted feeding nor periodic fasting address the basic lack of nutrition our bodies receive in consuming today's overly-processed, nutrition-deficit diets. The question remained: What's the best way possible to achieve the important restorative process of autophagy without further exacerbating the under-nourishment we experience every day? This is what my experiments with Pat, Amy and Julianna were based on. As we will see, **Intermittent Blasting** has the potential for being the most optimized method we have for losing weight *and* staying healthy!

I ran into Pat a little while after our conversation and he had some interesting news. First, I could tell he was thinner. He had lost about fifteen pounds since I had seen him last. He told me that he and his wife had followed this program for two days per week over two months and had achieved their weight loss goals. Julianna operates a med spa and shared this technique with her clients who experienced incredible results with both weight loss and an improvement in a wide variety of health markers. The results were amazing, and with my history with fasting and detoxing I knew the benefits went way beyond a simple loss of weight. Next, I knew I had to address the issue of the basic lack of nutritional value in the foods we eat today so that our fasting can be optimized.

The solution to the malnourishment problem was to create an entirely new way of looking at intermittent fasting that would specifically include foods that were 1) extremely high in nutrient density and quality, and 2) very easy for the body to digest and assimilate so it can quickly get back to the work of restoration and fat burning quickly. Most of my research up to this point had focused on the benefits of the fasting aspect. But the results I was seeing with my friends made me think harder about the side of the equation that involved superfoods and the amazing nutrition they bring.

Intermittent Blasting: A Simple Solution

Simply put, Intermittent Blasting combines intermittent fasting and superfoods (a "blast" of nutrients). This allows the body to rid itself of toxins while promoting fat burning and weight loss while "blasting" the body with as much high-quality nutrition as possible. This nutrition feeds our body what it has been missing in the Standard American Diet (SAD) of nutrient-deficient processed foods. It keeps us active, alert and full of energy while allowing the body to, rest, rejuvenate, burn fat, and rid itself of toxins.

Plus, with Intermittent Blasting you can STOP counting calories and trying to adhere to strict lifetime limits on certain food groups; *and* stop popping diet pills or staying within long-term narrow and unrealistic meal plans. Intermittent Blasting fits our modern lifestyles. As we will discuss in the following chapters, you can eat normally on non-Blasting days and still receive the health benefits and weight loss you desire!

The biggest challenge with Intermittent Blasting is how to know exactly what to consume on your "Blasting" days. When you consume less than seven-hundred calories a day you want to include as much high quality nutrition as possible. But what type of protein, carbohydrate and fat are best to use? Most people are already lacking in nutrients to some degree and by lowering your caloric intake you are by default lowering your nutrition even more. That's where the Blast of nutrients comes in.

The following chapters will explain in detail just why Intermittent Blasting works so well and how it suits the design and natural function of our bodies. Clinical trials with intermittent fasting in both animals and humans are confirming positive results with weight loss and compliance as well as improvements in a wide variety of health markers. Intermittent fasting is a vital part of how our bodies heal, cleanse and control weight. We have lost sight of this important fact in a world surrounded by 24/7 food options. But as recently as three generations ago, we still lived in feast-and-famine cycles common to human societies for thousands of years, to which our bodies naturally adapted.

We also know our brains are hardwired to binge whenever we can so we can weather the coming famine. But today, no famine ever comes. Junk food surrounds us all the time and it's cheap, easy and devoid of nutrition. We crave food all the time, because periodic famine is all our bodies have known for all but the last two or three generations. The very idea of fasting without being forced by some external force (bad weather, burned crops, lack of wild game to hunt) is difficult to accept. It takes will power for us to fast the way our ancestors did. But remember, their conditions forced them to fast where we must make the choice to do it on our own. Intermittent Blasting makes this one of the easiest diet choices you'll ever make.

The Revolution Starts Now!

Think of Intermittent Blasting as a day spa for your cells. Rather than superficially pampering your skin and nails, Intermittent Blasting cleanses your body from within while blasting your cells with highly nutritious, easily digestible and absorbable nutrition. This allows your cells, tissues, and organs time to rest and rejuvenate, leaving you refreshed and energetic – all while burning unwanted fat.

It seems that one thing everyone notices after starting Intermittent Blasting is how much food has been controlling them throughout their lives. You begin to realize how habitual food is and how much time and effort goes into the whole process of food preparation, shopping or deciding on a restaurant. We seem to be predisposed to always be thinking about what and where we are going to eat. Intermittent Blasting not only resets your physical system, it resets your mental attitude towards food, teaching us how much modern society has taught us to overeat.

Consider every day of Intermittent Blasting an accomplishment, as you are one step closer to your weight loss goal. Each day you are reinforcing your weight loss. Weight management is finally within your control. Intermittent Blasting is truly a revolution in healthy weight loss. With this protocol, you can achieve your weight loss goals, keep the weight off, and be healthier than you have been in years.

Looking back, I was struck with how intermittent fasting has allowed me to manage my own weight over the years. I have experimented with a wide variety of fasting and cleansing regimens, ranging in duration from one day to three weeks, using water, vegetable juice and fruit juices. And I have utilized a variety of herbs and natural products to assist the body with detoxing and cleansing.

Today, I've settled into a fairly consistent pattern. Every other week I fast for one or two days and a few times per year I fast for six-seven days. I have done this solely as a benefit to my overall health and wellbeing, but I also discovered in addition I've noticed how easy it has been to maintain my ideal weight. It had not occurred to me until recently to attribute this to intermittent fasting.

PART II: WHY WE NEED INTERMITTENT BLASTING

Chapter 4: Obesity in America

When we talk about obesity, there are two primary concepts we need to consider when it comes to the food we eat: quantity and quality. People talk a lot about quantity and no doubt, it's a big factor. But the quality of the food we eat is also a major contributing factor. While we eat more and more quantity, the quality of our food – which is the nutritional value our bodies take in and the resultant health benefits– has steadily declined. We have created a situation the human race has never dealt with before. We are malnourished even as we routinely consume more calories. We are literally eating ourselves   into   nutrient   deprivation.

Obesity In America

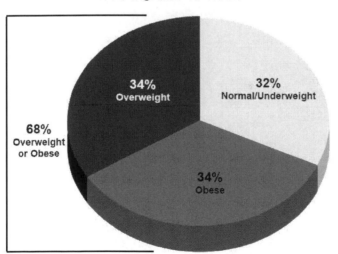

31

What is Obesity Anyway?

First, many people confuse the terms overweight, obese, and what is sometimes referred to as morbid obesity. Morbid obesity is extreme weight caused by both environmental and genetic factors. For discussion purposes, we will use the formal definition of "obese," and it's not as heavy as you might think.

The Centers for Disease Control and Prevention define obesity this way:

For adults, overweight and obesity ranges are determined by using weight and height to calculate a number called the "body mass index" (BMI). BMI is used because, for most people, it correlates with their amount of body fat.

An adult who has a BMI between 25 and 29.9 is considered overweight.

An adult who has a BMI of thirty or higher is considered obese.

By this definition more than two-thirds of Americans are currently overweight (68 percent) and over more than one-third are obese (34 percent). Overall, the percentage of adults more than twenty years of age who are considered obese is up from twenty-two percent in 1994 to thirty-four percent in 2008.

We have a real crisis in America. Obesity is truly an epidemic and it is causing untold suffering, ill health and tremendous financial burdens. For the first time in history, there are actually more people over age twenty who are overweight (approximately 1.5 billion) than those who are undernourished or hungry (approximately 1 billion). That's more people who are overfed than underfed.

But the personal health toll on our bodies tells only half the story. Obesity and the sickness and disease that stem from this condition are causing huge financial burdens on individuals, and the nation as a whole.

Next-Generation Obesity

U.S. Childhood Obesity

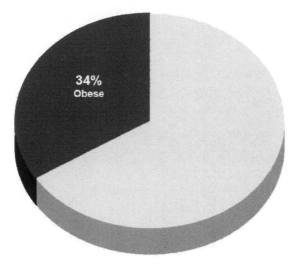

34%
Obese

It is not the adult population that is being hit hardest by the obesity epidemic. Our children are suffering more than ever before. Childhood obesity in children and adolescents has skyrocketed in the past thirty years.

The percentage of children ages 6-11 in the U.S. who are obese has more than doubled from seven percent in 1980 to nearly eighteen percent in 2010. The percentage of adolescents aged 12-19 years who were obese tripled from five percent to 18 percent during the same period. In 2010, more than one-third of children and adolescents were overweight or obese. This can be verified by the CDC here:

33

> ✉ http://www.cdc.gov/healthyyouth/obesity/facts.htm

For some perspective here, obesity rates for children stayed at or around the same level for most of recorded history. Even at the dawn of industrialization and modern food processing in the 1940s and 1950s, the rates were still only around five percent. Then, in as little as twenty years, these rates increased almost three-hundred percent. This is a radical shift which does not bode well for the future of our health, nor for our financial well-being.

Growth In U.S. Childhood Obesity
1980 - 2010

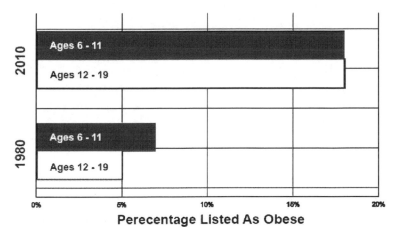

Perecentage Listed As Obese

Quantity of Food

For the first time in human history, we now have the ability to eat whatever we want whenever we want, twenty-four hours a day, three-hundred sixty-five days a year. Think about this for a moment. As recently as one-hundred-fifty years ago most of our consumption relied on what we could get out of the ground from a good harvest. A bad harvest meant a lot of people went hungry. Even as hunters, the wildlife we ate depended on the cycles of nature. Good years and bad years in weather and nature were cyclical. Our bodies were designed to weather these cycles by storing fat in good times and burning those fat stores in hard times.

The problem is that our bodies are geared to always expect the hard times – storing fat at every possible opportunity. But hard times, in relation to food consumption, no longer exist. When was the last time you looked at the sky and wondered if the weather would help you get enough to eat? When was the last time you pulled rotten crops from soaked fields and went home to tell your family that there would be no dinner?

The fact is, we have access to food around the clock. Whenever our bodies feel the slightest bit hungry we can satisfy that craving immediately. We've forgotten how it feels to be hungry... but more importantly, we have become afraid of hunger. "Hunger" has become a red-flag word --standing in for deprivation or starvation. Hunger is neither of these things. Hungry is, in fact, a good thing to be from time to time.

How much food do we eat?

The average American eats 29 pounds of French fries, 23 pounds of pizza and 24 pounds of ice cream annually. We consume 53 gallons of soda, 170 pounds of sugar, 24 pounds of artificial sweeteners, 2,736 grams of refined salt, and 90,700 milligrams of caffeine per year. All these are major contributing factors for obesity and ill health.

In America from 1971 through 2000 the average calorie consumption of women increased by more than 20 percent, from 1,542 calories to 1,877 calories. That's an additional 335 calories a day. Men increased their calorie consumption during the same period by 168, a seven-percent increase from 2,450 calories in 1971 to 2,618 calories in 2000.

Calorie Consumption 1977 - 2000

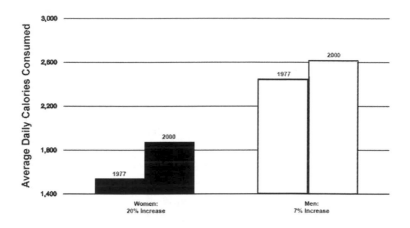

In her excellent book on the subject, Obesity: Breaking Through to The Thin Within, author Debra L. Zebari writes:

> *"Restaurant servings are about three times bigger than a normal portion size. Larger portions not only provide more calories, but studies show that when people are served more food, they eat more food (Young & Nestle, 2002). People shouldn't overeat when dining out simply because the food is there but we do. Over time, portion sizes have increased as our bodies have expanded."*

When comparing a Betty Crocker Cookbook written in the 1960s to one written more recently, the latter includes the same recipe with the same amounts of ingredients, but instead of feeding four-to-six people the same recipe now feeds two-to-four.

In the 1950s, a "family size" bottle of Coca Cola was twenty-six ounces. McDonalds' original burger, fries and a twelve-ounce coke provided 590 calories. Today a super-sized Extra Value Meal, with a Quarter Pounder with Cheese, super-sized fries, and a super-size coke delivers 1,550 calories as documented by the National Alliance for Nutrition and Activity, or NANA, in 2002.

The National Institute of Health backs up this conclusion with the following hard data:

> ☰ http://www.ncbi.nlm.nih.gov/pubmed/23885112

Mean portion size in calories increased significantly by 21 percent ($\beta = 0.63$; $p < 0.01$) over the past 100 years in the analyzed recipes. The mean portion size in calories from a composed homemade meal increased by 77 percent ($\beta = 2.88$; $p < 0.01$). The mean portion size in calories from meat increased by 27 percent ($\beta = 0.85$; $p = 0.03$), starchy products increased by 148 percent ($\beta = 1.28$; $p < 0.01$), vegetables increased by 37 percent ($\beta = 0.21$; $p = 0.13$) and sauce increased by 47 percent ($\beta = 0.56$; $p = 0.02$) throughout the years.

Cornell's Brian Wansink's study titled, "The Joy of Cooking Too Much" drew a similar conclusion. The study reviewed recipes in seven editions of The Joy of Cooking over a period of seventy years. Eighteen recipes appeared in each of the cookbooks, and of the eighteen, fourteen had an increase in calories of an astonishing 43.7 percent.

> ☰ http://foodpsychology.cornell.edu/outreach/joy-of-cooking.html

And we are eating constantly. We eat non-stop from the time we get up until the time we go to sleep. From 1977 to 2006 the time between eating or snacking has decreased by an hour for both adults and children, confirmed by data at:

http://www.ncbi.nlm.nih.gov/pmc/articles/PMC2854907/

The good news is that technological advancements in food production allowed us to finally break free of thousands of years of binge-and-starve cycles that nature dished out so we can have a virtually unlimited food supply all day, every day. The bad news is that our bodies are still geared to eat as if we are going to starve soon. So, it's clear that as food becomes more and more available to us, our bodies are wired to eat more and more of it. As we continually eat and eat our bodies are hard at work storing fat in preparation for a rainy day that never arrives. It's no wonder we are becoming obese at alarming rates.

Chapter 5: Overweight and Starving

The Decline of Food Quality

You would think that having enough food to eat is a positive thing. This is something that we have been striving for throughout human history. But there is a very strange thing happening. It turns out that one of the primary challenges people face who are overweight is that they are malnourished. That's right…obese people are both *OVER*weight and *UNDER*nourished. Seems implausible, right? How can someone who is fifty or even one hundred pounds overweight possibly be malnourished?

Our rate of expansion in industrialized food manufacturing and distribution during the past fifty years seems staggering when compared to the rest of the history of humans on earth. This is quite an accomplishment. As a result, today in the U.S. and most developed nations, products are refined and preserved in such a way as to remain "fresh" for months and years as opposed to days, and there are virtually no limits imposed by the seasons in grocery stores. You can purchase food products (even produce) year-round, regardless of your local climate, as these foods may have been grown halfway around the world in perfect growing conditions and shipped to your local grocery.

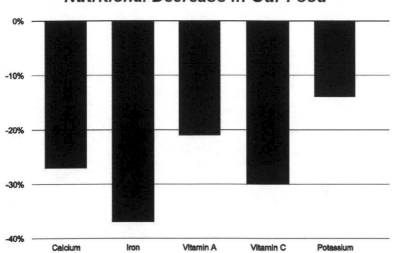

Nutritional Decrease In Our Food

However, these new processes strip our food of the vital nutrients we need to survive. In their place, we find added chemicals, preservatives, artificial sweeteners and genetically modified organisms. Food has become less nutritious than what we used to pull out of the ground, and more of something created in a lab designed to stay fresh forever and tickle our senses of taste and smell. The sad fact is the vast majority of "food" consumed in America today is practically void of nutrition.

When Food Stopped Being Food

Concurrent with our rise in obesity, cancer, heart disease and diabetes, has been an unprecedented advancement in food production,

39

storage and distribution. I call this entire process "Industrialized Food Production," and it is the machine that is responsible for the vast majority of the food that reaches our tables today. From the very soil in which the plants grow, to the containers in which they are shipped, no part of the process is spared chemical treatment. Our food is washed, bleached, sucked dry, deconstructed, reconstituted, preserved, frozen and reformed. All this requires a host of chemical processes. In addition, our food travels an average of 2,000 miles from ground to table, which creates two problems: first, the produce must be harvested long before it has fully ripened, which allows less time for it to receive all of the nutrients from the soil that it would otherwise have absorbed. Second, food begins the process of losing nutrition from the moment it is picked, so the farther it travels, the less nutrition it will contain when it finally arrives.

As a result of these modern manufacturing practices, the majority of our "food" doesn't resemble the food on which our ancestors thrived. In fact, our great-grandparents would not even recognize the majority of "foods" or what might more accurately be described as "food-like products" or "non-foods" that reside on the inside aisles of most major grocery stores in the U.S.

My grandparents were farmers in rural North Carolina. As a child, I remember my grandfather taking me to his greenhouse (or "hothouse" as he called it) where he would grow his fresh vegetables. He was always very excited to see how well they were doing and was always eager to show them to me. When my cousins and I wanted an afternoon snack we would pick grapes from the grapevine, an apple from the apple tree or go into the field and pick a cucumber, go inside and cut it up, put it in vinegar and add salt and pepper. When we were thirsty we would drink water straight from the ground beneath our feet.

Those days are gone for most Americans. The average American consumes well below the recommended eight servings of vegetables and fruit per day. Nowadays most kids grab a pre-packaged lunch, heat up some mac and cheese from a box or at best have a peanut butter and jelly sandwich. At worst, they eat tons of refined sugars in candy bars and other sweet treats. How far did these foods travel and what kind of processing did they undergo? It seems that our primary motivating factor in choosing the foods we eat is no longer quality, but convenience.

On my grandparents' farm, grapes, apples, and cucumbers straight from the garden were unrefined and unprocessed -- organic, with no added chemical preservatives, no trans fats, no high fructose corn syrup, and no MSG (monosodium glutamate). The water was fresh and full of minerals without poisons such as pesticide runoff, chlorine, fluoride and pharmaceutical residue. When comparing those types of foods to what we eat today, it's clear we are consuming a mere shell of what our ancestors ate and the food we eat contains many toxic chemicals that are making us sicker and sicker.

If we examine how our food is made today and compare it to food from one hundred years ago it should not come as a shock that coinciding with the rise of industrialized food production has been a similar rise in chronic disease. Yet so many of us seem unaware of the connection chronic disease and obesity.

Soil Fertility

The factors that rob our food of nutrition start before the seeds are even planted in the ground. Most food crops are grown in soil that has been depleted of vital nutrients. Modern conventional farming does not require rotation of crops to preserve soil quality. So, after growing the same crops in the same soil season after season the soil becomes depleted of vital nutrients. When the soil is lacking nutrients, the produce grown there will also lack nutrients. And if the produce lacks nutrients, when we consume it, we will lack nutrients.

41

As early as 1936, the U.S. Senate was presented with the results of a scientific study it had commissioned on the mineral content of our food. The results demonstrated that many human ills could be attributed to the fact that American soil no longer provided the plants with the mineral elements that are so essential to human nourishment and nutritional health. Imagine this happening more than seventy-five years ago!

Senate Document 264 of the 74th Congress, 2nd Session 1936, from the March 1936 issue of Cosmopolitan says:

"...99 percent of the American people are deficient in... minerals, and...a marked deficiency in any one of the more important minerals actually results in disease."

Do you know that most of us today are suffering from certain dangerous diet deficiencies that cannot be remedied until the depleted soils from which our foods come are brought into proper mineral balance? The alarming fact is that the fruits, vegetables and grains now being raised on millions of acres of land no longer contain enough of the minerals we need. So no matter how much we eat, our cells are starving for nutrition!

We know that vitamins are complex chemical substances which are indispensable to nutrition, and that each of them is important for the normal function of some special structure of the body. Disorder and disease result from any vitamin deficiency. It is not commonly realized, however, that vitamins control the body's appropriation of minerals, and that in the absence of minerals they have no function to perform. Lacking vitamins, the system can make some use of minerals, but lacking minerals, vitamins are useless.

Laboratory tests prove that the fruits, vegetables, grains, eggs and even the milk and meats of today are not what they were a few generations ago. No person today can eat enough fruits and vegetables to supply his or her system with the mineral salts he requires for perfect health.

It is bad news to learn from our leading authorities that ninety-nine percent of American people are deficient in these minerals, and that a marked deficiency in any one of the more important minerals results in disease. Any upset of the balance, any considerable lack of one or another element, however microscopic the body requirement may be, will sicken, suffer, and shorten our lives. Take a look at the Senate report cited here:

> http://www.dailypaul.com/92623/1936-us-senate-report-soil-depleted-99-of-americans-nutrient-deficient

The following is from a Scientific American article reporting on a landmark study conducted in 2004 by Donald Davis and his team of researchers from the University of Texas (UT) at Austin's Department of Chemistry and Biochemistry:

> *"Efforts to breed new varieties of crops that provide greater yield, pest resistance and climate adaptability have allowed crops to grow bigger and more rapidly but their ability to manufacture or uptake nutrients has not kept pace with their rapid growth." There have likely been declines in other nutrients, too, he said, such as magnesium, zinc and vitamins B-6 and E, but they were not studied in 1950 and more research is needed to find out how much less we are getting of these key vitamins and minerals.*
>
> *The Organic Consumers Association cites several other studies with similar findings: A Kushi Institute analysis of nutrient data from 1975 to 1997 found that average calcium levels in twelve fresh vegetables dropped 27 percent; iron levels 37 percent; vitamin A levels 21 percent, and vitamin C levels 30 percent. A similar study of British nutrient data from 1930 to*

1980, published in the British Food Journal, found that in twenty vegetables the average calcium content had declined 19 percent; iron 22 percent; and potassium 14 percent. Yet another study concluded that one would have to eat eight oranges today to derive the same amount of Vitamin A as our grandparents would have gotten from one.

... They studied U.S. Department of Agriculture nutritional data from both 1950 and 1999 for 43 different vegetables and fruits, finding "reliable declines" in the amount of protein, calcium, phosphorus, iron, riboflavin (vitamin B2) and vitamin C over the past half century.

☰ http://www.scientificamerican.com/article.cfm?id=soil-depletion-and-nutrition-loss

Davis attributes the decline of nutrients in our soil to modern agriculture practices that increases plant size, growth rate, and resistance to insects. So not only is the soil more depleted of vital nutrients but the fact that crops grow faster and larger can also result in less time for the plant to absorb the nutrients.

Clearly our food has less of the actual nutrients it is supposed to contain. When you don't get the nutrients your body requires, it just keeps asking for more by giving you hunger and cravings. You just keep eating more and more and are never satisfied. It's an endless cycle. Sound familiar?

Food Processing

The act of processing and refining the foods consumed by the majority of Americans strips them of vital nutrients. The following example pertains to a wide variety of commonly-consumed foods such as white bread, white pasta, white rice, most sugars and the list goes on and on, to include anything made of white flour like cookies, cakes, crackers, cereals etc.

Let's look at wheat. Whole grains consist of three parts: bran (outer layer), endosperm (middle layer), and germ (inner layer). During the refining process, the bran and germ are completely striped away and only the endosperm is left. The endosperm consists primarily of starchy carbohydrates and is low in nutrients. The bran and germ contain the majority of nutrients like fiber, vitamins, minerals and antioxidants.

Putting the whole grain puzzle together: health benefits associated with whole grains

It is estimated that the refining process reduces the fiber content by eighty percent and greatly reduces levels of minerals, vitamins and phytonutrients as cited here:

> ✉ https://www.ncbi.nlm.nih.gov/pubmed/21451131

The refining process that strips food of vital nutrients is such a concern that many governments (including our own FDA) require that refined products such as flour, pasta and rice be supplemented or enriched with synthetic B vitamins (thiamine, riboflavin, niacin and folic acid) and iron. So as a replacement for natural nutrients lost in the refining process, manufacturers are required to throw in synthetic chemicals totally void of the many enzymes and cofactors contained in the original nutrient, in a feeble attempt at replenishing what has been lost in the refining process.

What is a "cofactor"? Simply put, vitamins aren't meant to be consumed as individual components. Rather, they require a variety of supporting enzymes and minerals that exist in the plant itself to function fully in our bodies. For our bodies to optimally extract the nutrients contained in a food, many cofactors should be present. For example, there is a large and varied panel of cofactors contained in a single blueberry. Refined white bread has virtually none.

So why do food manufacturers do this? Because long-term shipping and storage demand it. Foods simply cannot exist in the industrialized food system in their natural form. They will spoil too quickly.

Proper Nutrition Comprises the Building Blocks for Health

Through the natural process of apoptosis, the average adult experiences the death of between fifty and seventy billion cells each and every day. So we must constantly provide our bodies with the building blocks necessary to rebuild and regenerate each of those cells on a daily basis. "Foods" like cereal, fries, pizza, mac and cheese simply do not contain the nutrition our bodies require to fulfill the demands to maintain optimal health.

It is only when food enters our bodies in its natural form that we are best able to receive the nutrition it offers. Overly processed, artificially preserved, and chemically altered "foods" don't allow us to extract proper nutrition because it simply does not exist in those products. An apple has more than 2,000 molecular structures that our bodies recognize as nutritional elements that serve as building blocks for our health. That single apple contains a great deal of nutritional information that our bodies utilize to perform a variety of sophisticated processes including nourishment, repair and regeneration. In today's world, through soil depletion and over processing, a lot of these nutrients are just plain missing.

So, what do we do? Many of us load up our bodies with synthetic vitamins created in a laboratory and think this will make up the difference. What we fail to realize is that our bodies do best when consuming a complex nutritional matrix with hundreds and even thousands of nutrients working in concert in their naturally occurring forms. Our bodies simply don't know what to do with synthetic vitamins and end up flushing most of them out with our urine. That is why our urine changes color when taking vitamins in a pill form. If you take vitamins as part of their naturally occurring matrix in, say, an apple or mango, your urine remains clear or slightly yellow.

The bottom line is that while we load up on empty calories, our cells are starving for nutrition, which makes us even more hungry. Our cells are screaming for more nutrients but all we do is pile on more empty calories. The cycle of hunger-binging-hunger increases, and this is how we become both obese and malnourished at the same time. The worst of both worlds!

This industrialized processing is not limited to the grains and other plants we eat. Essentially the same can be said of the manufacturing process for our animal products.

Ironically, truly "empty" calories would be better for us than the type of calories most people consume which are loaded with chemicals; including pesticides, herbicides and pharmaceuticals such as antibiotics. Livestock consumes nearly 80 percent of the antibiotics used in the U.S. When we consume these animal products we are also consuming chemical residues.

There is a vast difference between wild game when compared to factory farmed, mass-produced animal products. Wild game is much leaner and richer in omega three fatty acids than animals raised in large industrial farms. Additionally, products from factory farmed, mass-produced animals most often contain chemicals, such as nitrates, used as preservatives. The animals also consume growth hormones and antibiotics to lower feed costs and stimulate faster growth. This has been shown as a factor in weight gain.

☰ http://www.nytimes.com/2014/03/09/opinion/sunday/the-fat-drug.html

---

Additives, Preservatives and other Non-Food "Foods"

At this point, we've seen that the soil in which our food is grown is lacking nutrients. Then the refining process depletes nutrients even further. What else is done to our food that causes it to be less nutritious or even harmful? Over the course of time, the modern food industry has embraced a few additional practices that cause further harm to our foods. Introducing cheaply- manufactured ingredients such as Trans Fats, High Fructose Corn Syrup, and MSG (monosodium glutamate) serves to increase shelf life, enhance flavor and lower manufacturing costs. Unfortunately, they all come with harmful consequences.

All these products are man-made; meaning they don't occur naturally. As a result, our bodies don't quite know what to make of them. Best-case scenario is that they get flushed out with waste. Worst-case is that they too are a contributing factor in what is making us sick and overweight.

Partially Hydrogenated Oils (Trans Fats)

In recent years, you see a lot in the news about Trans Fats, and for good reason. Trans fats are very harmful to health. Trans fats are very difficult to digest and have been found to increase bad cholesterol (LDL), decrease good cholesterol (HDL), and have also been shown to cause a variety of diseases including heart disease and diabetes. Trans fats cause weight gain and have been shown to cause obesity and changes in insulin sensitivity in monkeys.

🗐 http://www.ncbi.nlm.nih.gov/pubmed/17636085

As if that isn't bad enough, trans fats also cause nutritional deficiencies. Trans fats are commonly found in margarine (which should never be used), cookies, cakes, chips and salad dressings. Many countries have strict regulations, if not outright bans, on trans fats, and in the U.S., several major cities such as New York, San Francisco, Chicago, and Philadelphia prohibit the use of trans fats in restaurants and other eateries. In the U.S., the FDA announced as of November 8th, 2013, an outright ban on trans fats, which forces food manufacturers to exclude the substance in foods consumed in the U.S. Putting an end to trans fats is a step in the right direction but we must resolve to do much more if we are to turn the tide of ill health and obesity. And I ask also, "What about the damage already done?"

High Fructose Corn Syrup (HFCS)

Excessive use of refined sugar is detrimental to bodily processes in many ways and can greatly increase the risk of diabetes and obesity. HFCS is a highly refined liquid sweetener alternative extracted from corn (now mostly genetically modified), and then chemically altered to yield a substance tasting like sucrose (common table sugar). It was first used in foods and beverages in the 1970s.

HFCS increases triglyceride levels and LDL (bad) cholesterol, can damage tissue in the digestive tract, and inhibits leptin, which is the hormone that signals that brain that the body is full and directs it to stop eating. The Coca-Cola company replaced cane sugar with HFCS in 1984 as a result of the U.S. government providing subsidies to corn farmers, ultimately incentivizing the replacement of cane sugar with HFCS.

In Mexico where there are no government subsidies to incentivize farmers to grow corn, Coca-Cola sweetens their beverage with an ingredient they once used in the U.S.: cane sugar. "Mexican Coke" has recently become popular in America. Users will pay twice as much for Mexican Coke because it contains real cane sugar as opposed to HFCS. Mexican Coke drinkers say it has a more "natural taste" and this is not surprising as cane sugar is natural and HFCS is not.

Professor Barry Popkin, PhD, in the Department of Nutrition, at the University of North Carolina in Chapel Hill, is an authority on the dangers of sugar-sweetened soft drinks and their link to obesity. Writing about HFCS in the American Journal of Clinical Nutrition he explains how fructose can contribute to obesity: "Consumption of high-fructose corn syrup in beverages may play a role in the epidemic of obesity. The digestion, absorption, and metabolism of fructose differ from those of glucose. Hepatic metabolism of fructose favors "de novo lipogenesis" (production of fat in the liver). In addition, unlike glucose, fructose does not stimulate insulin secretion or enhance leptin production. Because insulin and leptin act as key afferent signals in the regulation of food intake and body weight (to control appetite), this suggests that dietary fructose may contribute to increased energy intake and weight gain. Furthermore, calorically sweetened beverages may enhance caloric over-consumption." Check out the study and more from Popkin at: Bray, G.A., Nielsen, S.J., and B.M. Popkin. 2004. Am J Clin. Nutr. 79(4):537-43. Review.

> 🗐   http://www.ncbi.nlm.nih.gov/pubmed/15051594

Monosodium Glutamate (MSG)

MSG's can be found on product labels in more than forty different forms with hard-to-pronounce names straight from your high school chemistry class: maltodextrin, autolyzed vegetable protein, sodium caseinate, autolyzed yeast, hydrolyzed vegetable protein, yeast extract and citric acid.

MSG is considered a neurotoxin, excitotoxin and an anti-appetite suppressant (meaning it actually can make you hungrier). It can cause indigestion, stomach cramps and gas. MSG is used to induce obesity in laboratory rats since rats are not naturally overweight. It causes the pancreas to release too much insulin, which can lead to type 2 diabetes, and yes...obesity. Do you notice a pattern developing with these food additives?

In Spain, scientists saw a 40 percent increase in appetite by feeding MSG to mice. They concluded that the increase in appetite was due to the MSG affecting an area of the brain that prevents the body's appetite control mechanisms from functioning properly. The rats got hungrier the more they ate. Sound familiar?

> 🖅 http://www.euroresidentes.com/Blogs/2005/12/scientists-in-spain-link-additive-to.htm

Traditionally, MSG was known as an additive in Asian cuisine but today MSG's are virtually ubiquitous throughout the inner aisles of grocery stores and supermarkets. MSG's can be found in everything from diet beverages, fast foods, canned soups, hot dogs, sausages, salad dressings and even some vegetarian foods and nutritional supplements.

Misinformation, Both Purposeful and Not

I believe people generally want to make healthier choices for themselves and their families. However, there is so much confusion and misinformation disseminated by everyone -- from advertisers of consumer brands, to the media and the government (both which are heavily influenced by financial interests) to your brother-in-law or next-door neighbor -- that it's virtually impossible to know what to believe. Most often you just need to follow the money to find the culprit of misinformation.

Between the federal government being influenced by agriculture lobbyists, (wheat, dairy, meat, pork, corn and others), farmers being paid to plant crops and not to plant crops based on government subsidies, (also influenced by the big agriculture lobby), and consumer brands marketing their products, it's virtually impossible to receive non-biased nutritional information totally void of outside influence. Companies will do almost anything to get you to purchase their products. Food companies still tout the "low fat" phrase even though fat alone doesn't make people fat and never has. This is common knowledge among anyone who knows the first thing about nutrition, but it's such marketing magic it's still being exploited today.

So how did we get here so quickly? How did we replace the entire human history of food production and distribution in just the past several decades? That story has been well told by qualified investigative journalists. The following are excerpts of two excellent articles that take on this story and I urge you to take some time and locate the original source and read up on it.

Why Our Food Is Making Us Fat – The Guardian, June 2012

> 🖃   http://www.theguardian.com/business/2012/jun/11/why-our-food-is-making-us-fat

"Butz - a Nixon appointee - pushed farmers into a new, industrial scale of production, and into farming one crop in particular: corn. U.S. cattle were fattened by the immense increases in corn production.... As a result of Butz's free-market reforms, American farmers, almost overnight, went from parochial small-holders to multi-millionaire businessmen with a global market.

By the mid-70s, there was a surplus of corn. Butz flew to Japan to look into a scientific innovation that would change everything: the mass development of high fructose corn syrup (HFCS). HFCS was soon pumped into every conceivable food: pizzas, coleslaw, even meat. It provided that "just baked" sheen on bread and cakes, made everything sweeter, and extended shelf life from days to years...the food on our plates became pure science – each processed milligram tweaked and sweetened for maximum palatability. And the general public was clueless that these changes were taking place.

In 1984, Coke in the U.S. swapped from sugar to HFCS (In the UK, it continued to use sugar). As a market leader, Coke's decision sent a message of endorsement to the rest of the industry, which quickly followed suit...especially as there were no apparent health risks. At that time, "obesity wasn't even on the radar" says Hank Cardello Director of the Obesity Solutions Initiative.

The food industry had its eyes on the creation of a new genre of food, something they knew the public would embrace with huge enthusiasm, believing it to be better for their health - "low fat"... But, says Lustig, there was a problem. "When you take the fat out of a recipe, food tastes like cardboard, and you need to replace it with something – that something being sugar."

The Extraordinary Science of Addictive Junk Food by Michael Moss – New York Times, Feb 2013

> http://www.nytimes.com/2013/02/24/magazine/the-extraordinary-science-of-junk-food.html

"What I found, over four years of research and reporting, was a conscious effort — taking place in labs and marketing meetings and grocery-store aisles — to get people hooked on foods that are convenient and inexpensive."

Chapter 6: The Costs of Obesity

The Health Costs of Obesity

I hear some people make this argument from time to time: So we are a few pounds heavier than we were thirty years ago. Doesn't this mean there is finally enough to eat for everyone? Isn't this what we were striving for as a society?"

If you look up "obesity" on Wikipedia, you will find that, "Obesity is a leading preventable cause of death worldwide... and authorities view it as one of the most serious public health problems of the 21st Century." The website, WebMD is more specific:

The health problems associated with obesity are numerous. Obesity is not just a cosmetic problem. It's a health hazard. Someone who is 40 percent overweight is twice as likely to die prematurely as a normal-weight person. Obesity has been linked to several serious medical conditions, including:

- *Heart disease and stroke*
- *High blood pressure*
- *Diabetes*
- *Cancer*
- *Gallbladder disease*
- *Gallstones*
- *Osteoarthritis*
- *Gout*
- *Breathing problems*
- *Sleep apnea*
- *Asthma*

Doctors agree overwhelmingly that the more overweight a person is, the more likely he or she is to have health problems. People who are overweight or obese are at increased risk for chronic disease compared to normal-weight individuals. People who are overweight or obese can gain significant health benefits from losing weight. A person is considered obese if he or she weighs at least 20 percent more than the maximum healthy weight for his or her height, according to Web MD.

The CDC agrees and adds the following conditions to their list of obesity-related illnesses: Stroke, type 2 diabetes, cancers, (such as endometrial, breast, and colon cancer), high total cholesterol and high levels of triglycerides, liver and gallbladder disease, reproductive health complications such as infertility and some mental health conditions.

So here we see a host of medical problems related to being overweight or obese that are detrimental to our lives. Let's look a little closer into some of the major categories here and what their impact is; not only on our lives as individuals, but on society as a whole.

Cardiovascular Disease/Heart Disease

One out of every three Americans die of cardiovascular disease. Heart disease is the number one cause of death for both men and women in the U.S., claiming approximately one million lives annually. Every thirty-three seconds someone in the U.S. dies from cardiovascular disease which is roughly the equivalent of a September 11th-like tragedy repeating every day, 365 days a year. This year, nearly one million Americans will have a heart attack; nearly half of them will occur without prior symptoms or warning signs. More Americans die of heart disease than of all kinds of cancers combined.

Cancer

Cancer is the second leading cause of death in the U.S. One out of every 2.2 Americans will develop some form of cancer in their lifetime. One person dies every minute in the U.S. from cancer. One in eight deaths in the world are due to cancer. Cancer causes more deaths than AIDS, tuberculosis, and malaria combined. In 2008, 7.6 million people died of cancer worldwide. By 2030, 21.4 million new cancer cases are expected globally, resulting in 13.2 million cancer deaths. It's estimated that 12,060 children in the U.S. are diagnosed with cancer annually and 1,240 will die from the disease.

Cancer rates for teenagers have increased by fifty percent over the last thirty years. According to the National Institute of Health (NIH), the cost of cancer in 2007 in the U.S. was $226.8 billion. Globally, the economic impact of cancer is substantially higher than that of any other cause of death. Most researchers believe that well over half of all cancers and cancer deaths are preventable.

Diabetes

Diabetes (primarily type 2) is at epidemic proportions in the U.S. According to the CDC (Centers for Disease Control and Prevention) fifty percent of American adults will be pre-diabetic or diabetic by 2020. A recent Morbidity and Mortality report (MMWR) released by the CDC shows that from 1995 to 2010, there was at least a hundred percent increase in the prevalence of diagnosed diabetes cases in eighteen states. Forty-two states saw an increase of at least fifty percent.

People living in the U.S. are three times more likely to have diabetes than people living in the United Kingdom. However, this epidemic is spreading globally as other countries embrace the Western lifestyle of fast food and sugary drinks.

China recently surpassed the U.S. in prevalence of diabetes, not only in sheer numbers but also as a percentage of population at 11.6 percent compared to the U.S. at 11.3 percent. In 1980, China's diabetes prevalence was below one percent. That's more than a 1,000 percent increase in less than thirty years.

Diabetes Rates In China 1980 -2013

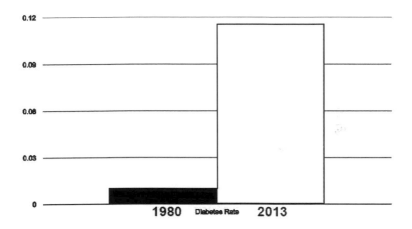

Overall Life Expectancy

In 1960, life expectancy in the U.S. ranked fifth in the world. In 2000 it had fallen to 24th, and by 2010, the U.S. was ranked 49th. Puerto Rico, an American territory, has a greater life expectancy than people living in the U.S. According to a report published in The New England Journal of Medicine, for the first time in two centuries the current generation of children in America may have shorter life expectancies than their parents.

A story in the New York Times says that obesity is so great, especially in children, that the associated diseases and complications - type 2 diabetes, heart disease, kidney failure, cancer - are likely to strike people at younger and younger ages.

> 📧 http://www.nytimes.com/2005/03/17/health/17obese.html)

Once again, the finger is pointed directly at obesity.

The Financial Costs of Obesity

Overall, our numbers on health care spending are both staggering and depressing.

According to the Centers for Medicare & Medicaid Services, health care expenditures in the U.S. were nearly $2.6 trillion in 2010, which amounts to an average of $8,402 per person. Americans spend more on health care than any other country, yet forty-eight countries have longer life expectancies than the U.S.

The U.S. spent more on health care in 2009 than the entire Gross National Product of Great Britain. If the U.S. health care system was a country, it would be the sixth largest economy in the entire world. Over the past decade, health insurance premiums have risen three times faster than wages in the U.S. Americans spend approximately twice as much as residents of other developed countries on health care.

More than half of all bankruptcy filings in the U.S. are due to illness or medical bills, according to the American Journal of Medicine, June 2009. By 2019, the U.S. is expected to double its health care expenditures to $4.5 trillion.

In 2008, overall medical care costs related to obesity for U.S. adults were estimated to be as high as $147 billion. People who were obese had medical costs that were $1,429 per year higher than the cost for people of ideal body weight. Obesity also has been linked with reduced worker productivity and chronic absence from work.

Chapter 7: Dieting Doesn't Work

Our food is nutritionally deficient, which makes our bodies want more of it, so we eat more nutritionally deficient food but the only thing we get from it is heavier and heavier and sicker and sicker. So, what can we do?

We go on diets. Tons of them. Dieting is a multi-billion-dollar industry in the U.S. We want a solution that is as cheap and convenient as the problem that put us here in the first place. There are more than 30,000 diet-related books listed on Amazon. Unfortunately, most diets simply do not work. Just as our bodies were designed to consume whole foods from nutrient dense sources, our bodies are also designed to manage weight in a very specific manner. Most diets ignore this biological fact and try to flim-flam us with results with little or no effort on our part. "Take this pill and lose thirty pounds!" Sound good? Well, that just isn't how we are designed.

Can We Break the Cycle?

We are bombarded with billions of dollars spent annually to get us to purchase products that may not be the best choice for our health. Food and beverage companies spend approximately two billion dollars annually marketing directly just to children. Of course, we always have options if we look beyond the marketing and the misinformation. But our lives today are built primarily around cost and convenience. And, although it's unhealthy and makes us sicker and sicker, industrialized food production is one thing beyond all else: convenient.

We have many influences working against us when it comes to consuming proper nutrition and warding off diseases such as obesity. Depletion of soil, the refining process, and food additives, all set the stage for a laundry list of diseases including malnutrition and obesity. On top of everything else the unfortunate reality is that the refining process of foods, and additives like HFCS and MSG, lower manufacturing costs, so consequently the foods that are most affordable are those that lack the greatest benefits to our health. And for the record, it is well documented that people in poor and minority communities have a much greater chance of being obese and suffering from obesity-related diseases like diabetes and heart disease.

Here again is a big conundrum with almost every weight loss plan. When you cut calories, it generally follows logically that you decrease nutrition, and increase hunger. And lowering the amount of nutrition can indeed result in a downward spiral that may lead to a laundry list of chronic disease.

If lack of quality nutrition reaching our cells is the culprit, then the solution is simple. Get more nutrition to the cells! But how can we receive more nutrition while cutting calories?

First, it's important to consume lots of foods that are high in nutrition while being low in calories. These foods are referred to as nutrient dense: foods with low energy density meaning less calories relative to volume. However, these foods can be difficult to find in our convenience-obsessed society. Any farmers market is packed with nutrient dense foods, but going to the farmers market is certainly not as simple as going to the corner store.

The cost of organic, pesticide-free produce can be prohibitive as well. As discussed above, the driving factor in industrialized food production is getting costs down and convenience up. Over the years as farms switched to industrialized practices it became more expensive and rare to find farms that use organic solutions. Organic was once the only option; now it is the rare exception. Even if we all know that in the long-term this more than pays off in living a healthier life, most people think more in terms of immediate goals, like having enough money to pay the mortgage and the rest of their monthly bills.

So, we are eating more and getting fatter while at the same time starving our cells of basic nutrition. The nutrient-dense foods we need are becoming harder to find and more expensive. Despite the local food movements gaining acceptance, our lives are not getting any simpler or cheaper to live so to some extent we need the convenience and cost-effectiveness of industrialized food production.

Are All Calories Equal?

Before we begin our discussion of the inherent lack of effectiveness of traditional diet programs, we must briefly touch on the concept of calories, and how not all calories are created equally. A typical hamburger weighs 120 grams and contains around 350 calories. A typical apple weighs 180 grams and contains 100 calories. But the nutritional value of an apple is by far greater than the hamburger. This excerpt from *World's Healthiest Foods* says it best:

> *"Let's take a quick example. Say you're low on vitamin E, and decide to eat a food that is not nutrient dense. A slice of run-of-the-mill white bread will give you about 1/10th of a milligram of vitamin E. This 1/10th of a milligram will cost you about 80 calories (the number of calories in a slice of many white breads)."*

> *Now let's compare this number and amount to a slice of 100 percent whole wheat bread. Whole grain products, like most*

61

whole foods, are nutrient dense. A slice of 100 percent whole wheat bread will cost you approximately the same number of calories (about 70-75 calories) but the vitamin E content will be substantially different. Instead of getting only 100 micrograms of vitamin E in exchange for your 70-80 calories, with 100 percent whole grain bread, you will get between 250 and 500 micrograms of Vitamin E. Or, to put it somewhat differently, you would have to eat between 2-1/2 and 5 slices of run-of-the-mill white bread to get the same amount of vitamin E as is found in one slice of 100 percent whole wheat bread. And those extra 1-1/2 to 4 slices would cost you as much as 320 additional calories.

Chapter 8: Why Dieting Doesn't Work

There are three reasons why diets do not work.

- First, diets slow the metabolic rate, which makes it more difficult to lose weight and maintain weight loss.
- Second, dieting causes our bodies to increase the production of the hunger hormone called "ghrelin," which signals the body to increase consumption.
- Third, the social pressures of modern society make it difficult to comply with any long-term calorie restrictions.

There needs to be a greater understanding about the way our bodies are designed to cope with calorie restrictions rather than with a personal shortcoming or "lack of willpower." Beating ourselves up about a supposed lack of will power only serves to depress us and in turn, makes us eat more.

The Human Body: Complex and Adaptable

Diets don't work because our bodies are designed to adapt to a wide variety of stressful situations. It's just been over the past one hundred years or so that we have had food available at our fingertips 24/7. Until the age of modern agriculture, refrigeration and preservatives, humans quite frequently went long periods of time without food. As a defense mechanism, our bodies are designed to store fat to be used as nutrition during lean times. Our metabolism slows so we burn less calories in case the drought lasts several days or even weeks. Our bodies are very smart and sophisticated and we are constantly adapting and adjusting to the fluctuations in our nutrition.

We are machines designed to live through famine. In the days when our bodies were evolving and adapting to wide swings in the availability of food, there would be a good harvest for six years and a bad harvest in the seventh year. And the only people who lived through the seventh year were the ones who were overweight. So, if you were able to watch your weight very nicely, you weren't here anymore. "We are survivors of the obese," says Stephen Bloom, a noted obesity expert.

I'm not sure our ancestral cavemen were "obese," but they certainly had to be extremely efficient at storing fat to allow survival during times when they were without food. Even up until the modern age, agrarian societies faced times where crops didn't flourish due to inclement weather among other factors and food was scarce as a result.

According to the author, nutritionist, and Longevity Hot Spot researcher, Sally Beare, the people of Hunza, Pakistan, still go long periods of time with very little food as the winter gives way to summer and food stores are depleted. Yet these people are some of the healthiest people on the planet. It's quite possible these forced periods of fasting have health benefits far beyond what we can imagine.

Consequently, when we adopt a traditional diet by reducing calories, over time our bodies adjust by slowing our metabolism and as a result it becomes more difficult to lose weight and almost impossible to keep it off. As we diet by restricting calories to lose weight only to gain it back and then diet again, our bodies adapt to that as well, and over time, it becomes even more difficult to lose weight. This becomes a vicious cycle that continues to repeat itself over and over again.

Here is a recent study that tries to explain this phenomenon of how calorie restriction diets actually make us gain weight in the long run. Then we will break down this research into everyday language.

Long-Term Persistence of Hormonal Adaptations to Weight Loss

⌨ http://www.nejm.org/doi/full/10.1056/NEJMoa1105816

Caloric restriction results in acute compensatory changes, including profound reductions in energy expenditure and levels of leptin and cholecystokinin and increases in ghrelin and appetite, all of which promote weight regain.

Caloric restriction results in a rapid, profound reduction in circulating levels of leptin and energy expenditure and an increase in appetite. Other effects of diet-induced weight loss include increased levels of ghrelin and reduced levels of peptide YY and cholecystokinin. Our study shows that after diet-induced weight loss, there are alterations in the postprandial release of amylin and pancreatic polypeptide and, more important, that changes in levels of leptin, ghrelin, peptide YY, gastric inhibitory polypeptide, pancreatic polypeptide, amylin, and cholecystokinin, as well as changes in appetite, persist for

12 months. In addition, these changes would be expected to facilitate regain of lost weight, with the exception of the change in the level of pancreatic polypeptide, which reduces food intake. However, our findings are consistent with a study of obese children in which levels of pancreatic polypeptide increased after diet-induced weight loss.

A greater-than-predicted decline in twenty-four-hour energy expenditure after weight loss also persists for one year or more after the loss in weight has been maintained. In obese rats with diet-induced weight loss, normalization of enhanced metabolic efficiency lags behind weight regain.

Taken together, these findings indicate that in obese persons who have lost weight, multiple compensatory mechanisms encouraging weight gain, which persist for at least one year, must be overcome to maintain weight loss. These mechanisms would be advantageous for a lean person in an environment where food is scarce, but in an environment in which energy-dense food is abundant and physical activity is largely unnecessary, the high rate of relapse after weight loss is not surprising.

Although short-term weight loss is readily achieved through dietary restriction, only a small minority of obese people maintain diet-induced weight loss in the long term. A multitude of hormones, peptides, and nutrients are involved in the homeostatic regulation of body weight, many of which are perturbed after weight loss. Whether these changes represent a transient compensatory response to an energy deficit is unknown, but an important finding of this study is that many of these alterations persist for twelve months after weight loss, even after the onset of weight regain, suggesting that the high rate of relapse among obese people who have lost weight has a strong physiological basis and is not simply the result of the voluntary resumption of old habits.

Study Shows Why It's Hard to Keep Weight Off

⊟ http://www.nytimes.com/2011/10/27/health/biological-changes-thwart-weight-loss-efforts-study-finds.html

For years, studies in obesity have found that soon after fat people lost weight, their metabolism slowed and they experienced hormonal changes that increased their appetites. Scientists hypothesized that these biological changes could explain why most obese dieters quickly gained back much of what they had so painfully lost.

*But now, a group of Australian researchers has taken those investigations a step further to see if the changes persist over a longer time frame. They recruited healthy people who were either overweight or obese and put them on a highly-restricted diet that led them to lose at least **10** percent of their body weight. They then kept them on a diet to maintain that weight loss. A year later, the researchers found that "the participants' metabolism and hormone levels had not returned to the levels before the study started.*

The results show, once again, Dr. Leibel said, that losing weight "is not a neutral event," and that it is no accident that more than ninety percent of people who lose a lot of weight gain it back. "You are putting your body into a circumstance it will resist," he said.

In this particular study, the participants were on a calorie-restrictive diet for the period of eight weeks. So, when the study mentions "caloric restriction" they are referring to calorie restriction for a period of eight weeks. Referring to "acute compensatory changes" they are simply saying that the participants' metabolisms adjusted or compensated to the lower calorie regimen. This is a huge problem for dieters. Basically, the body "compensates," or adjusts, to the lower calorie diet and even after an entire year the metabolism is still operating at a slower rate. So, on the one hand you just lost a great deal of weight, but on the other hand, because the body reacts and adjusts, it is now much more difficult to maintain the lower weight due to a slower metabolism, and it becomes much more difficult to lose unwanted weight in the future.

Ghrelin: Killing the Messenger

To compound the problem, the body produces more ghrelin, so the appetite increases. Ghrelin is referred to by endocrinologists as the "hunger hormone." It literally creates the sensation of hunger. Why do you feel the hungriest when you are dieting? The longer you restrict calories the more your stomach produces ghrelin.

Let's have another look:

"reductions in energy expenditure and levels of leptin and cholecystokinin and increases in ghrelin and appetite, all of which promote weight regain."

So, not only does the metabolism slow and remain slow for a year or more following the calorie restrictive diet, but the appetite actually increases. Now that's a double whammy if there's ever been one.

Lastly,

"alterations persist for twelve months after weight loss, even after the onset of weight regain"

This means that even when you get back to your original weight before you began losing weight, the metabolism does not ramp back up to the previous rate, but remains at the lower rate.

Does dieting make you fat? A twin study.

| ≡ | https://www.ncbi.nlm.nih.gov/pubmed/21829159 |

In this study from 2012 researchers studied 4129 individual twins to determine whether weight gain following frequent dieting was contributed to genetic factors or dieting itself. The researchers conclude "our results suggest that frequent IWLs (Intentional Weight Loss) reflect susceptibility to weight gain, rendering dieters prone to future weight gain". It's not that complicated. Dieting makes you gain weight in the long term because it slows your metabolism.

Now, considering this, is there any question why the vast majority of diets do not work? When calories are restricted, the metabolism slows and remains slow, which makes it difficult to lose or maintain the lost weight. And this is traditionally how people lose weight - by either cutting back on calories or replacing meals with something that often is not very nutritious. Even worse, the appetite increases because our bodies are producing more ghrelin so you are even hungrier than you were when you started dieting. This sounds like an impossible situation, does it not?

To illustrate this problem, I can relate a personal experience of one of my business associates. He recently underwent gastric bypass surgery and he was very excited about losing over one hundred pounds fairly quickly. However, to achieve his ideal weight, he still needs to lose an additional one hundred pounds. Unfortunately, his weight loss has slowed considerably. He now consumes only 1,500 calories a day, yet he is no longer losing weight. Why is this happening? As the research above shows, long-term calorie restriction slowed his body's metabolism to the point where he is no longer burning calories quickly enough. The problem he is experiencing even after having an extremely invasive surgery is the same that to some degree, all dieters face. The body adjusts by slowing the metabolism, making it more and more difficult to lose weight.

Diet Compliance

The third primary reason diets don't work is compliance. There is a reason "die" is in the word diet. Dieting oftentimes makes you feel like you are going to die. Replacing meals, counting calories, eating low carb, eating only rice or only vegetables; all of these are just not easy to comply with and all of them require major adjustments to our lifestyles. It seems that to have success with cutting calories or eating low carb or low fat, you almost have to become a nutritionist to know exactly how much of what foods to eat during the course of a day.

But some of this is not our fault. Our bodies do not want to "diet" and we are not designed for it. So, a host of physical changes that happen when we diet are triggers from millenniums of experience in feast/famine cycles dictated by nature. These physical changes cause very real mental perceptions of hunger and panic.

Traditional dieting is burdensome on your lifestyle because you have to maintain it over long periods of time. We are social creatures; we enjoy having meals with others. Have you ever been on a diet and want to attend a dinner or social gathering? Difficult, isn't it? We all have experienced this at one time or another. It's easy to arrange this one or two times, but long-term diets call for permanent lifestyle changes constricting what you can and cannot eat on a daily basis, forever.

So, it's no wonder that sticking to diets is difficult for us. At the same time as our bodies are sending us "panic" signals triggering a host of mental effects, we are taking a social hit as well. Dinners become lonely affairs and lunches are just sitting alone at your desk with a shake, salad or a bowl of rice.

All you have to do is look around to see if any of these traditional weight loss programs' "diets" are working. During the past thirty years obesity in the U.S. has tripled from fifteen percent to forty-five percent even as these fad diets rake in billions of dollars in revenue. These methods have proven to be somewhat successful for a short period but due to the reasons outlined above, given time, they all become epic failures.

A Quick Word About Cravings

To set the stage for this subject I'll start with a quick personal story. Years ago, I was meeting with my doctor, Maurice Werness, and I mentioned that when I passed a local ice cream shop it felt like I was being pulled in that direction. I have always loved ice cream and this particular shop had really good ice cream. During the conversation Dr. Werness referred to this as my "craving" for sugar. It had never dawned on me that this urge was a "craving." I just thought I naturally liked ice cream.

Growing up, I saw my grandfather suffer with diabetes, losing both legs and dying prematurely. My mother explained to me that diabetes was a result of eating too much sugar so from an early age I always tried to avoid it. But I really love ice cream and I also love chocolate. I know now that this was being caused by a lack of certain nutrients that my body was seeking out, or craving. It was not that I just naturally had a "sweet tooth."

So why do we have cravings?

A "craving" is our body's way of telling us we are missing something. Unfortunately, these signals can get crossed, especially in a society where the only way to satisfy cravings is to reach out for junk food. But cravings are indeed a sign of malnutrition.

Do you crave sugar, chocolate, salty or fried foods? If yes, then your body most likely is in a state of malnutrition and is very likely lacking minerals specifically. Let's take chocolate, for example. Chocolate has a very high magnesium content and if you are low on magnesium your body will signal for you to eat chocolate. Have you ever heard of a child playing in the sandbox who decides to eat dirt? Her mother has a fit and tells her not to put that in her mouth. Most likely the child's body is signaling minerals are needed and tries to eat a big handful of minerals to solve the problem. Until you consume a massive amount of high quality concentrated nutrition you will likely continue to struggle with cravings.

You Can't Out-Exercise A Bad Diet

Despite various exercise crazes that routinely sweep the country every few years, we are still gaining weight at an alarming rate. According to many studies, more exercise does not equate to any significant weight loss.

More people are running, biking, and exercising in other ways in hundreds of U.S. counties.

> healthmetricsandevaluation.org.

But the [rise in physical activity levels] trend has had little impact so far on stopping the rising tide of obesity. As physical activity increased between 2001 and 2009, so did the percentage of the population that was considered obese.

More aggressive strategies to prevent and control obesity are needed. Diet and changes in individual behavior are the key components.

Dr. Ali Mokdad, Professor of Global Health at IHME says that around the country, you can see huge increases in the percentage of people becoming physically active, which research tells us is certain to have health benefits. If communities in the U.S. can replicate this success and tackle the ongoing obesity impact, it will see more substantial health gains.

Dr. Christopher Murray, IHME Director says: "In spite of the fact Americans are actively biking, walking, and working out we are still gaining weight. It's clear that an increase in physical activity is not solving our obesity problems."

"As good as exercise is for you -- and please be clear that I realize how important exercise is to our health -- it is not the single solution to the problem of obesity that some claim it to be, especially in our children," he adds.

I like to say, "You can't out-exercise a bad diet." While elite athletes in their prime such as Olympic swimmer Michael Phelps might be able to wolf down fast-food, pizzas and cheeseburgers and still stay trim, most of us do not come close to approaching this level of physical activity.

PART III: SUPERFOODS + INTERMITTENT FASTING = INTERMITTENT BLASTING

Chapter 9: Intermittent Blasting: A Revolution in Healthy and Lasting Weight Loss

Intermittent Blasting is different from ordinary diets because it works in concert with the way your body is designed to function, it charges your body with nutrients to make you feel energetic while enabling lasting weight loss.

Intermittent Blasting – A Solution

As I outlined in the previous section, there are three main barriers to traditional diets:

1. The body's ability to adapt to long-term calorie restriction by slowing its metabolism.
2. The production of ghrelin, which is the "hunger hormone" that increases appetite.
3. The social pressures that make long-term compliance nearly impossible.

Intermittent Blasting addresses these barriers through our body's natural biochemical abilities and through scientifically-backed research into how we can put our bodies into the best mode for losing weight without slowing its metabolism, and by allowing us to live a normal culinary lifestyle for the majority of the time.

Intermittent Blasting Eliminates the Slowed Metabolism Effect

Intermittent Blasting greatly reduces the amount of time it takes to lose weight, by taking weight off over short periods of time. As opposed to the long-term calorie restriction required of most diets that slows the metabolism, Intermittent Blasting does not give the body's metabolism time for this compensation to take effect. The metabolism stays at normal levels, which is required to efficiently burn fat. This is a very important aspect of the Intermittent Blasting approach to weight loss and weight management. When the body is at normal metabolic levels, ghrelin is not produced, so the incessant hunger that is the hallmark of traditional diets does not come into play.

Intermittent Blasting Is Easy to Stick To

Let's say that somehow your metabolism didn't adjust and become slower, making it more difficult to lose weight and maintain your ideal weight. And somehow your hunger hormone (ghrelin) didn't become elevated and make you even hungrier than you were before. Let's say you were able to miraculously overcome these pre-programed physiological bodily functions.

Now, all things being equal, compared to dieting every day for the rest of your life, wouldn't you prefer to carve out a couple of days periodically to Blast the weight off and maintain the lost weight by Blasting even less frequently, and eating normally the majority of the time? Intermittent Blasting allows you to arrange your schedule around a few days here and there rather than every day for the rest of your life.

Another advantage of Intermittent Blasting is that you can achieve many of the benefits of fasting by allowing the body to rest and expend energy on cleansing and restoration while feeding your cells with a much-needed Blast of nutrition in an easily digestible form.

The biggest hurdle most people face is the mental adjustment of getting used to the idea of greatly restricting calories for a short period time. But adjustment to this shift is a perfectly natural dynamic, for which we have historically and naturally adapted as humans. Again, it is only recently that we have had 24/7 access to all kinds of foods.

Nutritional Blast + Short-Term Calorie Reduction

The average American consumes on average 2,200 calories a day. On your Blast days you consume 500-700 calories per day. As an example, on a two-day Blast consuming 600 calories a day, you create a calorie deficit of around 1,600 calories every day. That's a 3,200 calorie deficit in just two days. To create the same calorie deficit over the course of a week by dieting daily you would need to consume 457 less calories per day than your usual diet. That's the equivalent of skipping a small meal every single day.

When you Blast two days a week you will create a calorie deficit of 3,200 calories each week. So you could either Blast two days a week or cut your caloric intake by 457 a day. Again, this would be similar to passing on a small meal each and every day.

Utilizing nutritional components designed specifically to be digested with ease, Intermittent Blasting is both convenient and cost-effective. Intermittent Blasting is as easy as drinking delicious nutrient-dense beverages periodically throughout the day, and can save you money as well. When you add up the cost of your usual meals, snacks, sodas and coffee, oftentimes the cost is much greater than the price of your nutrition on your Blast days. So, while you are losing unwanted pounds you have a net GAIN in your wallet.

The Intermittent Blasting Regimen

The basic concept of Intermittent Blasting is simple:

Fasting

Consuming easily digestible foods while greatly reducing your caloric intake for short periods of time. This puts your body into cleansing and restoration mode, greatly increasing your body's requirement and ability to burn stored fat.

Blasting

Blasting is when you flood your body with as much high quality, nutrient rich food as possible.

This combination gives your cells a "Blast" of nutrition to keep you alert, focused and full of energy while simultaneously giving your digestive system a break. Energy normally required for digestion is routed to the functions of repair, regeneration and fat burning.

This allows the body to be in the optimal state to burn fat, manage weight, and assist with repair of cells, tissue, and organs. Regular Intermittent Blasting will create a new, healthier you, while avoiding the pitfalls that cause most dieters to regain lost weight.

That's it! On days you are not Blasting you eat normally with no other change in lifestyle. Adding superfoods greatly enhances your body's ability to heal and repair itself. While I definitely recommend moving towards a healthier diet all-around, studies show the benefits of intermittent fasting exist regardless of changes in dietary and lifestyle habits.

It's clear that even though on your Blast days you consume well below your usual amount of calories, you actually greatly increase many health-promoting components such as bioflavonoids, carotenoids, polyphenols, and anthocyanins.

Intermittent Blasting is a healthy way to manage weight

Many people are very wary or hesitant about the idea of fasting. They believe it to be dangerous or unhealthy. But just the opposite is true. As I have mentioned in this book, our bodies are designed to rest, rejuvenate and heal during times of food shortage. What we have done in our modern society is eliminate this most basic of functions that our ancestors have been accustomed to since history began. The results are disastrous, with skyrocketing rates of chronic illness paralleling the rise of industrial food production and 24/7 food availability.

The fact is that fasting is one of the healthiest things we can do for our bodies, and Intermittent Blasting is a powerful tool that helps us achieve our health and weight goals in our modern society. It also easily and conveniently puts the nutrition back in our diet that has been missing for most of our lives.

Chapter 10: Fast

Fasting Works!

To fully understand the tremendous health benefits of Intermittent Blasting it's important to gain a basic understanding of the benefits of fasting. It is important to realize that the many health benefits of fasting can not only help control weight and improve overall health they also can extend life.

Before we get to the nuts and bolts of the Intermittent Blasting form of fasting, we need to look at why and how our bodies are designed to respond positively to periods of fasting.

What Is A "Fast"?

Fasting can be a very powerful therapeutic process helping participants recover from mild to severe health ailments such as high blood pressure, heart disease, cancer, type 2 diabetes, arthritis, eczema, and a variety of gastrointestinal disorders just to name a few. Juice fasting or juice cleansing, where you drink only fruit and/or vegetable juice for a given period of time, has gained tremendous popularity in recent years. There are many other examples of types of fasts but for our purpose, let's consider the definition of "fasting" as allowing your digestive system to take a break by abstaining from solid food over a given period of time.

Fasting provides a period of concentrated physiological rest during which time the body can devote its self-healing capacity to mechanisms designed to repair and strengthen damaged organs. Among the many benefits of fasting, the process also allows the body to cleanse the cells of accumulated toxins and waste products. This is done through a process called autophagy, which we will discuss in detail later in the book. Often times other methods are utilized to stimulate detoxification such as herbs and nutritional supplements to cleanse various organs such as the liver and/or gallbladder, colon, lymphatic system and blood. Extended fasts require professional supervision and often take place at a spa, resort, or medical facility. Medical fasts are sometimes done at clinics or hospitals.

If this is beginning to sound slightly unusual, believe me, I understand. My first introduction to fasting was one of the most unusual experiences of my life. As I mentioned in the beginning, when I was struggling to get my body back to health after my skiing accident and subsequent pharmaceutical dependencies, I had gone off all drugs except the caffeine in sodas and coffee and I was interested in anything and everything that could possibly help me get to a better place with my health.

Keep in mind, I was raised in the South on the typical southern diet consisting of; fried ham, fried bacon, fried chicken, fried pork chops, fried vegetables...well, you get the idea. And all were washed down with extremely sweet tea. At that time, my idea of eating healthy was having fried okra and fried squash. That is where my mindset was when it came to a healthy diet. So, going from that background to not eating anything for a week followed by a diet consisting primarily of vegetables, fruit and a little fish (as our instructor had taught us) was just plain weird to me.

However, it was abundantly clear that over time fasting was working. After years of pharmaceutical dependence, I was getting healthier and stronger with every fast. Over time, fasting seemed less "weird" and more vital and eventually became a natural part of my life.

Fasting in History and Religion

Some may think of fasting in the strict technical sense, meaning abstaining from food and drinking only water over a designated period of time. However, over thousands of years, many liberties have been taken with the term, which most often means abstaining from some subset of food or drink over a specific period of time.

The King James Version of the Bible refers to "fasting" in numerous ways. In Luke 4.2, referring to Jesus, the writer says he "ate nothing during those days, and at the end of them was hungry." One would assume Jesus did drink water during this time. Acts 9:9 says "For three days Paul was blind, and did not eat or drink anything." Clearly here, Paul didn't eat or drink. And Daniel 1:16 says, "so the guard took away their choice food and the wine they were to drink and gave them vegetables instead." Here certain foods were limited, but not all food. In fact, based on this very Bible verse, today there is a very popular fast called "The Daniel Fast." In the modern version of The Daniel Fast you will find that you can eat fruit, vegetables and grains and only abstain from animal products, sweeteners, leavened bread, refined products, fried foods, solid fats and beverages (other than water).

Fasting is not mentioned exclusively in Christian writings either. Days of fasting occur in almost every Abrahamic religion from Yom Kippur in Jewish tradition to the Islamic Ramadan. In the East, fasting is an important part of Hindu tradition with certain days set aside for fasting every week. In fact, every major religious observation mentions some kind of fast from Taoism to Mormonism; Sikhs and Buddhists and Eastern Orthodox.

So, it follows that since fasting is such an integral part of every religion, there must be some basic human need for it. And in fact, there is.

Wellness practitioners have been incorporating the healing properties of fasting into their practices for thousands of years, since ancient times as old as written history itself. Hippocrates, Socrates, and Plato all recommended fasting for health recovery. In medieval times, there is this story of one of the pre-eminent fasting practitioners.

Alvise "Luigi" Cornaro lived from 1467 - 1566. According to Wikipedia, Luigi was a Venetian nobleman who wrote treatises on dieting, including Discorsi della Vita Sobria (Discourses on the Sober Life). Finding himself near death at the age of thirty-five, Cornaro modified his eating habits on the advice of his doctors and began to adhere to a strict diet. His daily initial self-allowance was fourteen ounces (about 400g) of solid food and seventeen ounces (about 500g) of wine. He later reduced his daily intake to no more solid protein than an egg. His first treatise was written when he was 83, and its English translation, often referred to today under the title, "The Sure and Certain Method of Attaining a Long and Healthful Life," went through numerous editions; this was followed by three others on the same subject, composed at the ages of 86, 91, and 95. The first three were published at Padua in 1558. They are written, says Joseph Addison, in the early 18th Century periodical, The Spectator (No. 195), "with such a spirit of cheerfulness, religion and good sense, as are the natural concomitants of temperance and sobriety." He died at Padua at age 98.

🔲	https://en.wikipedia.org/wiki/Luigi_Cornaro

So, fasting has been around a long time. But today it is often misunderstood and worse, looked upon by some people as "unhealthy" or dangerous (perhaps an idea subtly put forth by the food industry). In truth, our bodies are very well designed for fasting and not very well designed for dieting. This is the core principle behind Intermittent Blasting. Our bodies are designed to fast periodically in order for the body to rest, burn stored fat and heal itself.

Chapter 11: The Science Is In: Intermittent Fasting Works!

Intermittent fasting has been around since humans first roamed the earth and now it's a new "secret" weapon for improved health and weight loss.

Wikipedia defines intermittent fasting this way:

Intermittent fasting (IF) is an umbrella term for various diets that cycle between a period of fasting and non-fasting. Intermittent fasting can be used along with calorie restriction for weight loss.

It has been long believed that a low-calorie diet or "calorie restriction" is very healthy and good for extending life as long as you continue to take in a balanced, nutrient-dense diet. Calorie restriction without malnutrition has been shown to result in longer maintenance of youthful health and decelerate the biological aging process in yeast, fish, rodents, and dogs. This is the *periodic fasting* method we discussed earlier. We do not want to confuse this with "dieting" in which we restrict calories over a period of weeks, months or years from an already malnourished body.

Many believe intermittent fasting can increase lifespan in humans. In addition to *periodic fasting*, the window of time in which we consume our calories has an important impact. If you recall, *time restricted* methods of fasting like *The 8 Hour Diet*, allows eating as much as you want for eight hours per day and abstaining from food entirely for the remaining sixteen. The basic principle here is that you are giving your body a much-needed rest two thirds of the time. In cultures known for their longevity, people take their last meal of the day well before the sunset and then "break the fast" after sunrise. There is mounting evidence that this plays an important role regarding weight management, longevity and overall wellness.

Proven Health Benefits of Intermittent Fasting

Research shows that intermittent fasting helps extend life, regulate blood glucose, manage cholesterol, burn fat and more. The benefits of intermittent fasting have been well-documented to help people look better, feel better, control weight, live healthier and longer.

Intermittent Fasting Reduces:

- body fat and weight
- blood lipids (triglycerides and LDL cholesterol)
- blood pressure
- risk of cancer
- inflammation
- oxidative stress

Intermittent Fasting Increases:
- fat burning
- metabolic rate
- cellular repair (autophagy)
- growth hormone release

Intermittent Fasting Improves:
- appetite control (through changes in ghrelin)
- blood sugar
- cardiovascular function
- effectiveness of chemotherapy (allows for higher doses more frequently)

Mark Mattson of the National Institute on Aging, has researched the health benefits of intermittent fasting and the benefits of calorie restriction. Mattson concludes that there are several theories to explain why intermittent fasting is so effective.

"The one that we've studied a lot, and designed experiments to test, is the hypothesis that during the fasting period, cells are under a mild stress, and they respond to the stress adaptively by enhancing their ability to cope with stress and, maybe, to resist disease. There is considerable similarity between how cells respond to the stress of exercise and how cells respond to intermittent fasting."

So, in the same way our bodies respond by building muscle when stressed by exercise, stressing our bodies during a fast causes our cells to respond in a way that may help ward off disease. What Dr. Mattson is describing is a bodily process called hormesis. Hormesis is the body's response to low exposures of toxins and other events that cause stress, such as strenuous exercise. Apparently, short-term fasting causes a hormetic response as well.

83

Fasting Controls Weight and Improves Health Markers

Intermittent fasting helps us lose weight and maintain ideal weight without slowing our metabolism. By creating a calorie deficit of 1500-2000 calories per day (depending on your current diet) you can obviously lose weight but because you are losing the weight over brief periods of calorie reduction you are not causing your metabolism to slow. This is a very important aspect of intermittent fasting and Intermittent Blasting.

Here is a study confirming fasting to be an effective method of losing weight and improving health markers, many others can be found in the appendix.

The effects of intermittent or continuous energy restriction on weight loss and metabolic disease risk markers: a randomized trial in young overweight women.

The goal of this study should be of interest to us all. It was designed to compare intermittent fasting with Continual Calorie Restriction (typical low calorie diet) and tested a very wide variety of health markers including improvements in cholesterol (LDL and HDL), triglycerides, blood sugar, blood pressure, sex hormones, inflammation (C-reactive protein) etc. Here we see both calorie restriction and intermittent fasting are shown to improve a wide variety of factors that affect our overall wellness. And typically, it is believed that the compliance rate is higher with intermittent fasting.

The study concluded that intermittent fasting of two days per week compares favorably with a low calorie diet of every day and was more beneficial in improvements with insulin and insulin resistance.

https://www.ncbi.nlm.nih.gov/pubmed/20921964

RESULTS: Last observation carried forward analysis showed that IER and CER are equally effective for weight loss: mean (95 percent confidence interval) weight change for IER was -6.4 (-7.9 to -4.8) kg vs -5.6 (-6.9 to -4.4) kg for CER (P-value for difference between groups = 0.4). Both groups experienced comparable reductions in leptin, free androgen index, high-sensitivity C-reactive protein, total and LDL cholesterol, triglycerides, blood pressure and increases in sex hormone binding globulin, IGF binding proteins 1 and 2. Reductions in fasting insulin and insulin resistance were modest in both groups, but greater with IER than with CER; difference between groups for fasting insulin was -1.2 (-1.4 to -1.0) μU ml(-1) and for insulin resistance was -1.2 (-1.5 to -1.0) μU mmol(-1) l(-1) (both P = 0.04).

CONCLUSION: IER is as effective as CER with regard to weight loss, insulin sensitivity and other health biomarkers, and may be offered as an alternative equivalent to CER for weight loss and reducing disease risk.

Fasting Increases Human Growth Hormone and Lifespan

Routine periodic fasting is good for your health, and your heart, study suggests

Recent research conducted by Dr. Benjamin D. Horne, PhD, MPH, director of cardiovascular and genetic epidemiology at the Intermountain Medical Center Heart Institute, showed that fasting was responsible for an incredible 2,000 percent increase in human growth hormone in men and 1,300 percent in women. The human growth hormone stimulates growth, cell reproduction and regeneration, has been linked to longevity, and is often referred to as "the fitness hormone." It promotes muscle growth and boosts fat loss by increasing metabolism.

Additionally, the study concluded that there was a benefit to cholesterol levels as well:

Unlike the earlier research by the team, this new research recorded reactions in the body's biological mechanisms during the fasting period. The participants' low-density lipoprotein cholesterol (LDL-C, the "bad" cholesterol) and high-density lipoprotein cholesterol (HDL-C, the "good" cholesterol) both increased (by fourteen percent and six percent, respectively) raising their total cholesterol – and catching the researchers by surprise.

"Fasting causes hunger or stress. In response, the body releases more cholesterol, allowing it to utilize fat as a source of fuel, instead of glucose. This decreases the number of fat cells in the body," says Dr. Horne. "This is important because the fewer fat cells a body has, the less likely it will experience insulin resistance, or diabetes."

Fasting Reduces Incidence of Inflammation

In a recent study of overweight adults with moderate asthma participants lost eight percent of their body weight by cutting their calorie intake by eighty percent on alternate days for eight weeks. In addition, markers of oxidative stress and inflammation decreased, and asthma-related symptoms improved, along with several other quality-of-life indicators as is examined in the following article.

Alternate day calorie restriction improves clinical findings and reduces markers of oxidative stress and inflammation in overweight adults with moderate asthma.

Even more astonishing, Mark Mattson and his colleagues compared the effects of intermittent fasting against calorie restriction for weight loss, insulin sensitivity and other metabolic disease risk markers. Published in the International Journal of Obesity in 2011, this study found that intermittent fasting was just as effective as calorie restriction for improving all these issues, and slightly better for reducing insulin resistance. According to the authors:

> http://www.ncbi.nlm.nih.gov/pubmed/17291990

Both groups experienced comparable reductions in leptin, free androgen index, high-sensitivity C-reactive protein, total and LDL cholesterol, triglycerides, blood pressure and increases in sex hormone binding globulin, IGF binding proteins 1 and 2. Reductions in fasting insulin and insulin resistance were modest in both groups, but greater with IER [intermittent fasting] than with CER [continuous energy restriction].

Fasting for Diabetics

I am constantly being asked the question; Can diabetics benefit from intermittent fasting? The following study shows the benefits of intermittent fasting for diabetes. There are several others in the appendix, but the short answer is yes, absolutely diabetes can benefit greatly from intermittent fasting. With any medical condition (and especially for diabetics) be sure to consult your personal physician before trying any diet or exercise regimen. Losing weight (regardless of the method used) is one of the best things anyone who is diabetic can do to lower their blood sugar.

Intermittent Blasting for diabetics is a little tricky because greatly reducing calories on your Blast days will likely result in lower blood sugar. So you must monitor your blood sugar levels very closely. For this reason, I would recommend starting slower, perhaps just Blast over a period of one or two meals. Provided that goes well, work up to where you are Blasting for an entire day and then two days.

The effect of short periods of caloric restriction on weight loss and glycemic control in type 2 diabetes.

Two groups who utilized an intermittent fasting regimen achieved greater weight loss and improved blood sugar compared with participants on a traditional diet of 1500-1800 calories per day.

> 🖹 https://www.ncbi.nlm.nih.gov/pubmed/9538962

Periodic VLCDs (Intermittent Very Low Calorie Diet) improved weight loss in diabetic subjects. A regimen with intermittent 5-day VLCD therapy seemed particularly promising, because more subjects in this group attained a normal HbA1c. Moreover, the glucose response to a 3-week period of diet therapy predicted glycemic response at 20 weeks, and it was a better predictor of the 20-week response than initial or overall weight loss.

Fasting Has Anti-Cancer Properties

Fasts have been shown to inhibit and reverse cancer growth. It has been shown to "consistently improve survival" of animals in the lab and in human trials. Fasting could help combat cancer and boost the effectiveness of cancer treatments.

One study found that fasting slowed the growth and spread of tumors and cured some cancers when combined with chemotherapy.

It is hoped that this discovery will prompt the development of more effective treatment plans and further research is now under way. The latest investigation, published in the journal, Science Translational Medicine, found that tumor cells responded differently to the stress of fasting compared to normal cells. Instead of entering a dormant state similar to hibernation, the cells kept growing and dividing, in the end destroying themselves.

In the article referenced below lead researcher Professor Valter Longo from the University of Southern California says, "the combination of fasting cycles plus chemotherapy was either more or much more effective than chemo alone," and "The cell is, in fact, committing cellular suicide. What we're seeing is that the cancer cell tries to compensate for the lack of all these things missing in the blood after fasting. It may be trying to replace them, but it can't." Professor Longo and his team looked at the impact fasting had on breast, urinary tract and ovarian cancers in mice. Fasting without chemotherapy was shown to slow the growth of breast cancer, melanoma skin cancer, glioma brain cancer and neuroblastoma - a cancer that forms in the nerve tissue. Scientists found tumor cells responded differently to the stress of fasting compared to normal cells. In every case, combining fasting with chemotherapy made the cancer treatment more effective. Multiple cycles of fasting combined with chemotherapy cured 20 percent of those with a highly aggressive form of cancer while 40 percent with a limited spread of the same cancer were cured. None of the mice survived if they were treated with chemotherapy alone."

Professor Longo added: "A way to beat cancer cells may not be to try to find drugs that kill them specifically, but to confuse them by generating extreme environments, such as fasting, that only normal cells can quickly respond to."

🖹 https://news.usc.edu/29428/fasting-weakens-cancer-in-mice/

🖹 http://www.dailymail.co.uk/health/article-2098363/Fasting-help-combat-cancer-boost-effectiveness-treatments.html

Dr. David Jockers Interviewed in the Documentary, *The Truth About Cancer*

> 📧 https://www.youtube.com/user/thetruthaboutcancer

I am a big fan of intermittent fasting. It's something I do every day and I think it's a critical piece of a cancer-killing diet. So, for myself, you know really when we break down fasting I want all our readers to understand this. I look at a building phase and a cleansing phase. OK, our building phase is the time between our first meal of the day and our last meal of the day. So the typical American might eat at 8 A.M. and finish eating at 8 P.M. That's about a twelve- hour building phase, and the cleansing phase would be the time from our last meal to our first meal. That's like a 1-to-1 ratio. In our society, we've got so much toxicity that it's that much more important that we have a greater cleansing phase than building phase. I like to have anywhere from a 16-to-18 hours, and sometimes even a 24- hour cleansing phase on a regular basis....Intermittent fasting is a very, very powerful strategy that's been shown to improve brain function, improve lean body tissue so your percentage of muscles to body fat is higher and it's been shown to improve almost every aspect of your health. And so very, very profound when it comes to killing cancer cells in your body too.

Fasting and cancer treatment in humans: A case series report

> 📧 https://www.ncbi.nlm.nih.gov/pmc/articles/PMC2815756/

The six patients who underwent chemotherapy with or without fasting reported a reduction in fatigue, weakness, and gastrointestinal side effects while fasting. In those patients whose cancer progression could be assessed, fasting did not prevent the chemotherapy-induced reduction of tumor volume or tumor markers. Although the 10 cases presented here suggest that fasting in combination with chemotherapy is feasible, safe, and has the potential to ameliorate side effects caused by chemotherapies, they are not meant to establish practice guidelines for patients undergoing chemotherapy.

Fasting Is Good for the Heart

Intermittent Fasting combined with calorie restriction is effective for weight loss and cardio-protection in obese women

This study demonstrates Intermittent Fasting contributes to improvements in a wide variety of health markers specific to heart health.

Sixty participants were measured for fat mass and fat free mass by dual energy X-ray absorptiometry (DXA), blood samples were collected, plasma total cholesterol, direct LDL cholesterol, HDL cholesterol, and triglyceride concentrations as well as fasting plasma glucose were measured in duplicate. Insulin, C-reactive protein (CRP), homocysteine, adiponectin, and leptin were also assessed in duplicate. All of these measurements were taken at week 1, 3, and 10. And blood pressure and heart rate were measured in triplicate each week using a digital automatic blood pressure/heart rate monitor. In other words, these participants were studied very closely.

The 10-week trial consisted of two dietary phases: 1) a 2-week baseline weight maintenance period, and 2) an 8-week weight loss period. During the weight loss period participants consumed 30% of their calorie needs six days per week and consumed only 120 calories one day per week.

The results were amazing and what I found most interesting is that across the board the metrics were better with the participants who consumed their calories from liquid rather than solid food.

Body weight decreased more (P = 0.04) in the IFCR-L group (3.9 ± 1.4 kg) versus the IFCR-F group (2.5 ± 0.6 kg). Fat mass decreased similarly (P < 0.0001) in the IFCR-L and IFCR-F groups (2.8 ± 1.2 kg and 1.9 ± 0.7 kg, respectively). Visceral fat was reduced (P < 0.001) by IFCR-L (0.7 ± 0.5 kg) and IFCR-F (0.3 ± 0.5 kg) diets. Reductions in total and LDL cholesterol levels were greater (P = 0.04) in the IFCR-L (19 ± 10 percent; 20 ± 9percent, respectively) versus the IFCR-F group (8 ± 3 percent; 7 ± 4 percent, respectively). LDL peak particle size increased (P < 0.01), while heart rate, glucose, insulin, and homocysteine decreased (P < 0.05), in the IFCR-L group only.

CONCLUSION: These findings suggest that IF combined with CR and liquid meals is an effective strategy to help obese women lose weight and lower CHD risk.

Fasting Improves General Health

I always say "give the body time to rest and good things happen". Here are several studies that show how fasting intermittently improves a wide variety of health markers.

Short-term modified alternate-day fasting: a novel dietary strategy for weight loss and cardio protection in obese adults.

In this study, sixteen obese subjects (twelve women and four men) completed a 10-week trial of alternate- day fasting. For this study, alternate day fasting is defined as a caloric reduction of 25 percent on fasting days. Body weight decreased, percentage of body fat decreased, total cholesterol, LDL (bad) cholesterol, triglyceride levels and systolic blood pressure all decreased.

> 🗏 http://www.ncbi.nlm.nih.gov/pubmed/19793855.

The rate of weight loss remained constant during controlled food intake (0.67 +/- 0.1 kg/wk) and self-selected food intake phases (0.68 +/- 0.1 kg/wk). Body weight decreased (P < 0.001) by 5.6 +/- 1.0 kg (5.8 +/- 1.1percent) after 8 wk of diet. Percentage body fat decreased (P < 0.01) from 45 +/- 2percent to 42 +/- 2percent. Total cholesterol, LDL cholesterol, and triacylglycerol concentrations decreased (P < 0.01) by 21 +/- 4percent, 25 +/- 10percent, and 32 +/- 6percent, respectively, after 8 wk of ADF, whereas HDL cholesterol remained unchanged. Systolic blood pressure decreased (P < 0.05) from 124 +/- 5 to 116 +/- 3 mm Hg.

CONCLUSION: These findings suggest that ADF is a viable diet option to help obese individuals lose weight and decrease CAD risk.

Challenging Oneself Intermittently to Improve Health

> 🗏 https://www.ncbi.nlm.nih.gov/pmc/articles/PMC4267452/

To survive and reproduce, our ancestors spent most of their waking hours working to find food, either by 'grazing' on plants or by hunting animals. In many instances, the food supply was very limited and so there was a survival advantage for those who could tolerate and adapt to periods of food deprivation. One such adaptation is the metabolic shift from the use of glycogen stores in liver and muscle cells, to the mobilization of fatty acids in adipose cells and their conversion to ketones, an alternative cellular energy substrate (Longo and Mattson, 2014). Another interesting adaptation suggested by studies of animal models, is that cognitive function and stress resistance improve in response to intermittent fasting (Wan et al., 2003; Ahmet et al., 2005; Mattson, 2012a; Marosi and Mattson, 2014). Similarly, endurance running, such as is required to chase and kill a deer (Zimmer, 2004), not only strengthens the muscles and heart, but also improves brain function (Ahlskog et al., 2011; Mattson, 2012b; (Voss et al., 2013).

Intermittent Fasting Modulation of the Diabetic Syndrome in Streptozotocin-Injected Rats

https://www.hindawi.com/journals/ije/2012/962012/

Over thirty days, groups of 5-6 control or STZ rats were allowed free food access, starved overnight, or exposed to a restricted food supply comparable to that ingested by the intermittently-fasting animals. Intermittent fasting improved glucose tolerance, increased plasma insulin, and lowered Homeostatis Model Assessment index. Caloric restriction failed to cause such beneficial effects.

A periodic diet that mimics fasting promotes multi-system regeneration, enhanced cognitive performance and health span.

https://www.ncbi.nlm.nih.gov/pmc/articles/PMC4509734/

We show that alternating PF and nutrient-rich medium extended yeast lifespan independently of established pro-longevity genes. In mice, four days of a diet that mimics fasting (FMD), developed to minimize the burden of PF, decreased the size of multiple organs / systems; an effect followed upon re-feeding by an elevated number of progenitor and stem cells and regeneration. Bi-monthly FMD cycles started at middle age extended longevity, lowered visceral fat, reduced cancer incidence and skin lesions, rejuvenated the immune system, and retarded bone mineral density loss. In old mice, FMD cycles promoted hippocampal neurogenesis, lowered IGF-1 levels and PKA activity, elevated NeuroD1, and improved cognitive performance. In a pilot clinical trial, three FMD cycles decreased risk factors/biomarkers for aging, diabetes, cardiovascular disease and cancer without major adverse effects, providing support for the use of FMDs to promote health span.

Fasting: Molecular Mechanisms and Clinical Applications

https://www.ncbi.nlm.nih.gov/pmc/articles/PMC3946160/

Based on the existing evidence from animal and human studies described, we conclude that there is great potential for lifestyles that incorporate periodic fasting during adult life to promote optimal health and reduce the risk of many chronic diseases, particularly for those who are overweight and sedentary. Animal studies have documented robust and replicable effects of fasting on health indicators including greater insulin sensitivity, and reduced levels of blood pressure, body fat, IGF-I, insulin, glucose, atherogenic lipids and inflammation. Fasting regimens can ameliorate disease processes and improve functional outcome in animal models of disorders that include myocardial infarction, diabetes, stroke, AD and PD. One general mechanism of action of fasting is that it triggers adaptive cellular stress responses, which result in an enhanced ability to cope with more severe stress and counteract disease processes. In addition, by protecting cells from DNA damage, suppressing cell growth and enhancing apoptosis of damaged cells, fasting could retard and/or prevent the formation and growth of cancers.

There is much more research to support the idea that a variety of fasting regimens are beneficial. I encourage you to turn to the Appendix and look into some of the research that has been done in this area. It is both extensive and compelling.

Conclusions – Fasting is Nature's Way of Maintaining Ideal Weight and Healing

Through my research and personal experience with the benefits of fasting I have discovered some key concepts:

1. The body is designed to heal itself and is constantly working to reach a state of homeostasis. Fasting can greatly assist the body in healing by focusing its energy on repairing and restoration rather than digestion.
2. Fasting is a natural part of life and one that is required for a longer, healthier life.
3. Intermittent fasting may be as effective as long-term fasting and is less difficult to implement and maintain.
4. It's easier for most people to restrict their eating intermittently than to decrease their calorie intake on a consistent, ongoing basis.
5. Proper nutrition is a key element in fasting. According to Dr. Stephen Freedland, Associate Professor of Urology and Pathology at the Duke University Medical Center, "undernutrition without malnutrition is the only experimental approach that consistently improves survival in animals with cancer."

Chapter 12: Superfoods

The key to Intermittent Blasting is to add highly nutrient dense food to our bodies while resting the digestive tract. These "superfoods" are rich in the nutrition our bodies need. They include exotic fruits and vegetables such as acai berries and noni fruit as well as more common examples like kale, spinach and apples.

This creates the amazing effect of "Blasting" our cells with nutrition while we give digestion the "day off." The resulting condition is like a day spa for your cells. The energy normally used for digestion is now more quickly diverted to restoration (including the cleansing process known as autophagy) while at the same time the body is being fueled with highly concentrated, bio-available nutrition.

Blasting the Cells with Superfoods Takes Fasting to the Next Level

While fasting is great for giving the body a much-needed rest, most people are so depleted of quality nutrition on the Standard American Diet (SAD) that fasting is not ideal because they are already in a nutrient depleted state. We've already discussed in the previous chapters how we can be both overweight and malnourished at the same time. Superfoods contained in smoothies, raw juices or fermented supplementation replenishes the body's functional reserves of nutrition for it to do the things it was designed for: energy creation, rejuvenation and weight management.

Intermittent Blasting gives the body a much-needed rest while blasting the cells with high quality concentrated nutrition. The amount of high quality nutrition received while on an Intermittent Blast from specific nutritional components such as bio-flavonoids, polyphenols, carotenoids and anthocyanins is vastly greater than what people are accustomed to receiving on a daily basis even while eating 2,500 calories of solid food. Think nutrient content, not calorie content.

The key to the nutrition on an Intermittent Blast is that it is easily absorbed and utilized by the body. The nutrition used for Intermittent Blasting is extremely easy on the digestive tract, taking very little time and expending very little energy to digest so the body can quickly return to the much-needed task of fat-burning, restoration and recovery. Intermittent Blasting gives the body a blast of concentrated nutrition without requiring the use of very much energy for digestion. It's simple, safe, and reduces the unpleasant detoxifying effects traditional fasting can produce, especially considering our current state of toxicity.

Those who Blast intermittently report increased energy, alertness, focus and loss of weight. Most people lose between two to six pounds in just the first two days. Plus, as an added benefit, they are healing their bodies by resting the digestive tract.

Smoothies and Juicing with Superfoods

Fruits and vegetables have a fibrous, "tough" cell wall that must be broken down to digest and utilize the nutrition. This begins to happen to some extent as we chew our food (one of the reasons chewing thoroughly is so important) and happens to a greater extent when blending into a smoothie or juicing, and to an even further extent through the process of lacto-fermentation.

Juicing has become a national phenomenon lately and it's no wonder why. Fresh pressed raw, organic juice is basically gourmet liquid nutrition and is very easily assimilated. You receive virtually all the nutrition without having to expend the digestive energy to separate the nutrition from the fiber. It's in a liquid form that is virtually "pre-digested" so the nutrition easily nourishes the cells.

Organic, fresh, cold-pressed juices work well because they retain the majority of the plants' nutritional elements and introduce very little in the way of additional sugars or sweeteners, which can interfere with the benefits of your Intermittent Blasting. Cold-pressed juices of this kind are available for purchase in most large metropolitan areas as well as online or you can juice the vegetables and fruit yourself at home. Be wary of processed juice, even the ones labeled "natural" or "organic" as they are not nearly as nutritious as cold-pressed juice.

Smoothies are a simple and economical way to incorporate superfoods into your Blast. Just throw your favorite mix of fruits and vegetables into a blender and you are on your way. It's quick and easy and does not involve the cost or mess of juicing.

Superfoods and Fermentation

Fermentation is an ancient process originally used for preservation of food that was common as recently as in our grandparents' day and still common in Longevity Hot Spots. However, fermentation has all but disappeared in the modern world due to the advent of chemical preservatives and refrigeration.

Fermentation enhances the nutrient content of foods in several ways. Nutrients such as vitamins and minerals are made more bioavailable as the plant's outer cell wall is broken down by the process, and additional nutrients are created as well. A good example of enhanced nutrient content is cottage cheese. Cottage cheese contains up to five micrograms of folic acid per one hundred grams, compared with the milk it is fermented from, which only contains one-fifth that amount. Therefore, through fermentation, foods are much easier to digest and also contain more nutrition. Fermented vegetables and fruit in powdered form are also "pre-digested" and assimilated very quickly and easily, and are a perfect complement to Intermittent Blasting.

Chapter 13: Cleansing – An Additional Benefit of Intermittent Blasting

How does "cleansing" happen? To fully appreciate the importance and impact of Intermittent Blasting, it's good to have a basic understanding of the complexities of the human digestive process. Digestion is a complex process requiring synergy from several different organs, including the stomach, small and large intestines, pancreas, liver and gallbladder. Digestion also utilizes a variety of components (some of which are contained in food and some of which are produced in the body) like enzymes, probiotics, acids and even hormones. The process of digestion requires a lot of energy and can be quite burdensome on the body. Just think about a Thanksgiving meal for example. When you eat that big Thanksgiving meal what happens next? You find yourself stretched out on the couch because your body now must focus its energy on the complex process of digestion.

Here's a fun fact: The human gastrointestinal tract is basically a thirty-foot tube beginning at your mouth and ending... well we all know where it ends. The surface area, if we were to lay it out flat, is enormous. Its total surface area is enough to cover an entire tennis court! Our GI tract is where we absorb our nutrients during the process of digestion and this requires a great deal of energy - especially when consuming a modern diet of highly-processed, highly-refined foods.

The Thermic Effect

The thermic effect is the term used to explain the amount of energy used in digestion, absorption, and distribution of nutrients. There is a different "Thermic Value" associated with each and every food. Digestion is one of the most difficult processes the body performs. It demands a tremendous amount of energy and in the case of proteins combined with certain foods, the process can take several hours. Due to the fact that we don't see it and it doesn't make us winded, we are largely unaware of the energy consumption that digestion demands. The process of digestion actually takes a significant amount of energy. We have to consider the net gain of the foods we consume. The net gain is what the body receives after the food has been processed for energy. The body receives energy from food by consuming a variety of nutrients. However, the more energy

100

the body expends to process the nutrition in the food we eat, the less nutrition actually reaches the cells, which is where it is needed.

On average, it is estimated that about ten percent of our overall calories are expended in the digestive process. And different nutrients require more or less energy to process. Protein requires twenty to thirty percent while carbohydrates take five to ten percent and fats less than one percent.

All nutrition prescribed for Intermittent Blasting has a very low overall thermic value. Therefore, your body is not expending any unnecessary energy and extracts the maximum amount of nutrition. While you are doing an Intermittent Blast, you will notice that your energy and alertness can actually increase. This is due in part to the reduced thermic effect of the foods you are consuming during your Blast.

Toxicity

In today's world it is virtually impossible to avoid toxicity. We have fluoride, chlorine and pharmaceutical residues in our water supply; mercury in our teeth; pesticides, herbicides, fungicides, and GMOs (genetically modified organisms) in our food supply; emissions and radiation in the air we breathe; and the list goes on and on.

We also receive toxicity from consuming animal products as a result of the toxicity they were exposed to in their environment as well as in their food and water supply. Livestock consume nearly 80 percent of antibiotics in the U.S., and they are often injected with growth hormone to increase productivity, and both are very toxic.

Researchers estimate the average person to have a minimum of 700 known toxins in their liver, blood, skin, brain tissue, fat tissue, digestive tract and other organ systems. This toxicity can accumulate in your body in your fat tissues (which is another reason not to carry extra weight).

Primary forms of toxins that affect us are contaminated water, smog and petrochemicals, pharmaceuticals, pesticides, solvents, fuel, parasites, formaldehyde, industrial exposures, tobacco, alcohol, sugar, and food preservatives. Toxins include heavy metals such as mercury, aluminum, lead, and cadmium, and bacteria like streptococcus, staphylococcus, and salmonella (food poisoning).

The body can also create toxins. For example, mucus can accumulate in the colon after having been produced as a byproduct of improper digestion that could be caused by consuming toxic foods. It can become quite a vicious cycle.

Here is a list of common symptoms of toxicity. Do you suffer from any of these?

- Dry eyes
- Dry skin, rashes, eczema or skin problems in general
- Heartburn
- Gas
- Constipation
- Diarrhea
- Fatigue
- Muscle aches
- Joint pain
- Sinus congestion
- Postnasal drip
- Excessive sinus problems
- Headaches
- Bloating
- Trouble sleeping
- Difficulty concentrating
- Trouble losing weight

- Canker sores
- Acne
- Puffy, dark circles under the eyes
- Bad breath

There was a time when I experienced almost all these at once.

The body is constantly working to preserve health and strives to reach a state of balance or homeostasis. The body's first defense when exposed to toxins is to eliminate them through one of the primary channels of elimination: the urinary tract, colon, lungs, skin, and the mucosal linings of the nose and ears. As toxins begin to accumulate in various organs they place severe stress on these processes of elimination. Continued accumulation will cause these systems to malfunction, setting the stage for a variety of abnormalities ranging from weakening of the immune system to cancer.

The body creates symptoms such as a skin rash, cough, diarrhea, congestion and nasal discharge for the purpose of protecting itself against toxins. During the process of cleansing these symptoms are commonly referred to as "detox symptoms" or can be called a "healing crisis." When toxicity makes its exit it can potentially produce these symptoms of detoxification.

As an example, when the body eliminates caffeine, symptoms usually include headaches, nervousness, and shakiness. When protein, meats, and fats are eliminated, you may experience skin eruptions, foul body odor, or a coated tongue.

> 🖹 http://drhyman.com/blog/2010/05/19/is-there-toxic-waste-in-your-body-2/

"We are exposed to six million pounds of mercury and...2.5 billion pounds of other toxic chemicals each year. Eighty thousand toxic chemicals have been released into our environment since the dawn of the industrial revolution, and

very few have been tested for their long-term impact on human health. And let me tell you, the results aren't pretty for those that have been tested ..."

"How can we not be affected by this massive amount of poison?"

"According to the nonprofit organization Environmental Working Group, the average newborn baby has 287 known toxins in his or her umbilical cord blood."

Dr. Mark Hyman, Is There Toxic Waste in Your Body?

Detoxing

Most people spend a great deal of their time and effort cleaning their external environment by washing their bodies, clothes, houses and cars but never consider cleaning their internal environment such as the liver, blood, skin, kidneys, digestive tract, etc. The volume of toxicity we are exposed to in today's world can cause our digestive systems and eliminative organs to malfunction, which can lead to degenerative or chronic disease. Therefore, it is important that we cleanse internally and assist the body to detoxify to help alleviate symptoms and reverse the damage caused by consuming herbicides, pesticides, genetically modified material as well as many other toxic substances.

Cleansing allows our over-burdened internal organs time for physiological rest and rehabilitation. This frees up energy to enhance the healing process. Along with a nutritious diet and balanced lifestyle, cleansing and detoxifying the body gives us a fighting chance by gently releasing and sweeping away toxic residues that have accumulated over time. Cleansing the body can provide relief from a variety of symptoms. In a matter of days most people report feeling refreshed, with clarity of mind as toxicity leaves their body. Ridding the body of toxic material restores energy and vitality.

Cleansing and detoxing has become much more widely accepted in recent years. However, some in the Western medical profession still do not recognize the accumulation of toxins in the body as problematic to health. Their position is that the body is perfectly capable of eliminating toxins on its own and is specifically designed to do so. In their defense, the accumulation of most of these toxins cannot yet be measured by conventional diagnostic methods, which is why some doctors deny their existence.

The alternative view to this (and the one I firmly believe and subscribe to) is that although the body is clearly designed to deal with toxicity, in today's world we are bombarded by so much toxicity that we are simply overwhelmed. Not to mention the fact that we now experience toxicity that our bodies have never experienced and were not designed to endure.

Challenging the Status Quo

The medical establishment has a long and storied history of clinging to the status quo and not being open-minded to change. We have a great example of this in Dr. Ignaz Semmelweis.

Dr. Semmelweis was a Hungarian physician practicing at the Vienna General Hospital in the mid-1800s. He was a pioneer in antiseptic procedures. He was puzzled by the much higher rate of puerperal fever among women and newborns in the hospital where he worked. One day a colleague was accidentally poked by a scalpel used on cadavers and subsequently died from the same puerperal fever.

Semmelweis immediately proposed a connection between cadaveric contamination (germs from a scalpel used on a cadaver) and puerperal fever. His theory was that medical students carried "cadaverous particles" on their hands from the autopsy room to the expectant mothers in the birthing room. Semmelweis discovered that the incidence of puerperal fever could be reduced drastically by the simple act of hand washing. He convinced the hospital to institute a strict policy that amounted to hand washing between procedures and the mortality rate instantly dropped 90 percent.

It's important to remember that in 1847 the germ theory of disease had not yet been postulated. The medical establishment at the time considered Semmelweis a lunatic and convinced his wife to have him committed to an asylum where he died two weeks later of septicaemia. It wasn't until 1862 when Louis Pasteur developed the germ theory that explained Semmelweis's findings that his theory gained widespread acceptance.

| ☰ | https://en.wikipedia.org/wiki/Ignaz_Semmelweis |

What seems perfectly logical and acceptable today was radical and suspicious when it was first proposed. I view cleansing in the same light. I firmly believe that in 10 or 20 years, cleansing will be an accepted part of mainstream medical practice.

Like the medical establishment's' reaction to Dr. Semmelweis, when I was first introduced to the concept of cleansing and detoxifying the body I thought it was the craziest thing I ever heard. After all, I had seen some of the very best medical specialists in the world and none of them had ever said anything about toxicity or cleansing. I remember thinking, "Let's say I have all sorts of toxicity in my liver, gallbladder, colon and other organs. And let's say I can cleanse it all out of my system. How can that possibly affect my skin, eyes, digestion, immune system, energy and all those other things?"

Well now I ask the opposite question. How can you expect your skin, eyes, digestion, immune system, energy and everything else to perform optimally if your primary organs are filled with toxic material? I am certain that most Americans are not experiencing optimal health as a direct result of their organs not functioning as designed due to accumulated toxicity.

Autophagy

In 2016 the Nobel Prize in Physiology or Medicine was awarded to Yoshinori Ohsumi for his groundbreaking work in the process known as autophagy, finally legitimizing the concept that the body is in a mode of cleansing when not digesting food. This is a concept I learned many years ago during my first forays into fasting.

> ≡ https://www.nobelprize.org/nobel_prizes/medicine/laureates/2016/press.html

Oshumi discovered the underlying mechanisms of autophagy and explained how the process worked. Autophagy is a cannibalistic process whereby the cells consume and recycle unnecessary or dysfunctional cellular components. This serves a dual function by allowing cells to survive during long periods of starvation (by basically eating the unnecessary components for energy) and it also serves as a cleansing mechanism. The cells generate energy by consuming unneeded and discarded material.

But the body cannot enter this process while digesting food. I learned in my research years ago that the body is constantly in one of two states: digesting or cleansing. It is never doing both at the same time.

Think of autophagy as your body's internal equivalent to the robot vacuum cleaner "Roomba." It's just going about its daily activities without you having to think about it. This is literally your body cleansing at the cellular level, and is required for health restoration. But autophagy can't happen when we are digesting. Digestion requires too much energy.

Autophagy is turned on and off by the simple act of eating. When you are digesting you are not in an autophagic state and when you are not digesting you are always in an autophagic state. It's as simple as that.

Most people in the U.S. are literally digesting food around the clock, from the time they get up in the morning until well after they are asleep at night. If you want to assist your body to cleanse and repair itself, you must give it time to do so by avoiding the complex process of digestion and allow the incredible process of autophagy to occur.

For example, I eat an early dinner, don't eat anything after dinner and I always start my day with fresh juice or a smoothie. This allows more time for my system to rest and recuperate. A vegetable and fruit juice or smoothie is a good way to break the fast (breakfast) every day because it is easy on the digestive track and will assimilate quickly so your body can get back to the work of cleansing. So, each day I have a few hours following supper to complete my digestion for the day and then I switch to a state of autophagy. I remain in an autophagic state until I have my juice or smoothie in the morning and since they are easily digested I return to an autophagic state quickly for a short time before lunch.

Some believe that autophagy plays a major role in longevity and is the reason why intermittent fasting can possibly extend life.

> 🖹 http://www.ncbi.nlm.nih.gov/pubmed/16874025

More research is needed but it seems that Autophagy can play an important role in supporting recovery from a variety of ailments ranging from bacterial and viral and cancer to neuronal diseases like Alzheimer's and Huntington's.

> 🖹 http://www.ncbi.nlm.nih.gov/pmc/articles/PMC151440/

Genetically Modified Organisms (GMOs)

A discussion of toxicity would not be complete without mentioning Genetically Modified Organisms (GMOs) and more specifically Genetically Modified Foods. Today GMOs are in 80 percent of the U.S. food supply so it's almost impossible to completely avoid them.

Independent animal studies have shown organ damage, gastrointestinal and immune system disorders, accelerated aging, and infertility from the consumption of GM foods. Human studies have shown how GM food can leave material inside the human body, possibly causing short-term and long-term damage. Genes inserted into GM soy can transfer into the DNA of bacteria living inside humans, and the toxic insecticide produced by GM corn has been found in the blood of pregnant women and their unborn fetuses.

Numerous health problems have increased after GMOs were introduced in 1994. The percentage of Americans with three or more chronic illnesses doubled, from 7-13 percent, from 1996 to 2005; food allergies have skyrocketed, and disorders such as autism, digestive disorders, reproductive disorders, and a host of others are on the rise. Organizations made up of doctors such as the American Academy of Emergency Medicine (AAEM) advise not to wait before protecting ourselves, and especially our children who are most at risk.

> http://www.reuters.com/article/2009/01/06/us-usa-chronic-idUSTRE5050S920090106

The American Public Health Association and American Nurses Association are among many medical groups that condemn the use of GMO bovine growth hormone, because the milk from treated cows has more of the hormone IGF-1 which is linked to cancer.

The majority of the corn, soybeans, cotton, sugar beets and rapeseed (canola) grown in the U.S. is genetically modified. In addition, a genetically-engineered growth hormone, recombinant bovine growth hormone, is widely injected in cows to boost milk production.

The best way to avoid GMOs is to avoid products containing corn, soy, sugar and canola and purchase only organic foods. A food product cannot be considered organic if it contains ingredients that have been genetically modified. For the record Monsanto, DuPont, Dow Chemical, Bayer, and Syngenta are currently the key players in the GMO market.

Chapter 14: Eat Normally

How many times has this happened to you? You start off on a new diet with the best of intentions. You want to lose weight, get healthy and feel better about yourself. Maybe you have to carefully count your calories every day to keep your weight at a certain limit. Maybe you have "two shakes and a sensible meal" every day. Maybe you have the dreaded weekly "weigh-ins" to go to each week. Maybe you are eliminating entire food groups from your diet every day.

So, you stick with it for a little while... maybe for a couple of weeks or even a month or two, and you're doing pretty well, maybe even losing a bit of weight. But then something inevitably comes up... a family function, an office picnic, or your birthday. You fall off your diet... once, twice... and then the next thing you know you forget to count those calories, and you are tired of those weekly trips to "weigh-in" where you get depressed because you aren't doing better, or you start craving foods you are told to avoid. You stop your diet and then what happens?

All that weight you worked so hard to lose comes rushing back - and then some. Soon you realize you weigh more than you did when you began your diet.

Social Pressures

We don't live in a bubble. We are social creatures and we love to interact with others. Connection is healthy! In our society we do that mostly over food -- dinner with friends, picnics, barbecues, and office luncheons. How many times have you been on a diet and attended one of these functions? You feel as though something is missing when you can't eat certain foods, especially the ones you really enjoy. You are counting and measuring everything you eat or sipping a shake while everyone else talks about how they are enjoying their delicious meal.

Social pressures are a big factor in why people fall off their diets. Never mind that these diets might not be good for you in the first place. When we find a diet that we think we can "stick to," we always run up against that social barrier where our self-imposed restrictions tempt us to "fall off" our diet.

The problem with most traditional diets is that they force you to alter your eating habits for the long-term, even for life. That's very difficult, and in fact might not be all that healthy. Keeping track of calories, weekly meetings, deprivation from the types of foods we love... it's no wonder these diets fail nine out of ten times.

The Joy of Eating Normally

Studies have shown that when you are on a program of intermittent fasting you receive tremendous health benefits regardless of your "normal" diet. Research in both laboratory animals and humans suggests that blood pressure, blood sugar and cholesterol all can be reduced when consuming less than 700 calories a day on an intermittent basis. Of course, I hope you maintain a healthy diet when you are not Blasting, but even if you don't, or if you want to splurge once in a while, you are getting a tremendous benefit to your health from the days you Blast.

111

That's one of the amazing aspects of Intermittent Blasting. It always fits in with your lifestyle. You get to choose your Intermittent Blasting days to fit around your schedule. The rest of the time you can eat normally. I will always encourage you to eat healthfully but that is ultimately up to you. You can enjoy family dinners, special occasions and work functions without fear or guilt. You don't have to constantly track calories of everything you put into your mouth. When you are not on your Intermittent Blast you can eat normally and still receive tremendous health benefits.

If you are committed to getting healthy and losing weight, the first thing you have to do is find two consecutive days that you can set aside for your first Blast. Look at your calendar and commit to those two days. Make sure there are no birthdays or work functions or other potential roadblocks; choose days in which your schedule is fairly routine. You will find that you will feel so good and you will be so excited about the weight you have lost, you will even look forward to doing it again. In fact, I've even had to tell some people to slow down. They get so excited about losing weight that they want to add more and more days but let's keep to the program outlined in the next section of this book.

The rest of the week, eat normally. Have lunch with your spouse, picnic, and grill out with friends for the big game. You don't have to worry about what you are eating or keep track of how much. Enjoy your life and your social functions guilt-free. I have found that when you can eat normally most of the time and make incremental changes in your diet at your pace, you become much more adaptive to creating positive habits that can last a lifetime.

Once you have completed your first Blast, you can choose your Blast days as you wish. Depending on your goals, you can extend your Intermittent Blasting days or reduce them to one day. You can plan your Intermittent Blasting days around your calendar. With traditional diets, the diet is in control of your life...with Intermittent Blasting you have complete control.

So, are you ready? Will you take the plunge and begin Intermittent Blasting today?

The next chapters will help you on your journey to better health. The following program is what produces optimal results with Intermittent Blasting. Hang on... you won't believe how quickly the weight will melt away and how good you will look and feel!

PART IV: BLASTING OFF!

Chapter 15: Getting Ready for Your Blast

Make it YOUR Blast

Your Intermittent Blasting regimen will be determined by your personal goals. Intermittent Blasting is very effective for weight management but is also great for cleansing, restoration and much more. As we discussed earlier in this book intermittent fasting has been shown to boost human growth hormone (HGH), increase testosterone, and improve the risk factors of inflammation, blood pressure, cholesterol, heart disease and cancer.

A typical one month schedule using Intermittent Blasting for maximum weight loss. Note that the Intermittent Blast days can be arranged to suit your individual schedule and goals. This is just one example of what your first month of Intermittent Blasting may look like for maximum weight loss.

You match your Intermittent Blasting days with your goals and lifestyle. If weight loss is your goal then you will Blast one way, while if you want to Blast for health and rejuvenation, you might take a different approach. Remember, a "Blast" is when you consume highly nutrient dense foods in an easily digested form, while decreasing caloric intake. Some people take five servings a day, others three and others as many as seven. Some choose to Blast for one to two days every week while others Blast for three to five days once per month. Some people Blast two days concurrently while others alternate Intermittent Blasting and eating days on an ongoing basis. Intermittent Blasting is flexible enough to fit whatever your goals may be!

Experiment! Choose the regimen that best suits your goals. The following are some examples of what I have seen and experienced through feedback of those who are having excellent results with Intermittent Blasting. Some people follow these regimens very closely for long periods of time, while others change their strategy often as their goals change. Intermittent Blasting is flexible enough to suit anyone's goals.

Getting Nutrition into Your Blast

There are two main features of the nutrition you should be consuming on your Intermittent Blasting days:

1. It should come from the most nutritious source possible, such as organic fruits and vegetables.
2. It should be easy to digest. Remember, we are trying to give our digestive system a break in order to get our body to focus on restoration and weight loss. Ideally it should be in liquid form and contain little or no protein.

There are many ways to obtain highly digestible liquid nutrition for your Blast. You can choose to stick with one or mix them up for variety. Remember Intermittent Blasting is flexible and you can tailor it to your lifestyle and goals. Some Intermittent Blasters prefer a specific regimen of the same beverages; others enjoy a bit more variety with their Intermittent Blast. In the companion book, *Intermittent Blasting Recipes*, there are additional smoothie, juice and soup recipes that are complementary and excellent for adding variety to your Intermittent Blast.

Smoothie Blast

Smoothies are ideal for Intermittent Blasting because they can provide you with powerful nutrition and fiber which is both filling and cleansing for the digestive tract. You can simply mix a variety of fresh or frozen fruits and/or vegetables in a blender with water, coconut juice or carrot juice and blend it up as fine as possible. I've included some of my favorite smoothie recipes later in this book, but the combinations are endless and you can tailor them to your tastes.

Cold-Pressed Juice Blast

One of the best beverages for your Intermittent Blast is fresh cold-pressed, organic fruit and vegetable juices. These juices pack a powerful nutritional punch; whether alone or as a base for nutritional supplementation. There are literally hundreds of combinations of ingredients to choose from to enhance flavor and variety. You can press these juices yourself if you are so inclined, or you can purchase them from a reputable source.

Nutritional Supplements

If you are working with a practitioner who prefers a particular whole food supplement that is easy to digest, or you have your own preference, you can consider using it, as long as it is whole-food-based and is not high in protein.

Supplementing Your Blast with Healthy Fat

It is also a good idea to include some healthy fat during your Intermittent Blast. Fats can be consumed in liquid form and added to your juice or smoothie recipe during your Intermittent Blast. These include nut milks, coconut oil, or blended avocado. Even fish oil or nut oil in tablet form will help to sustain and satiate you during your Intermittent Blast.

Avoid These!

You want to completely avoid anything highly processed or filled with sugar and chemicals even if it has the words "juice" or "all natural" on the label. Highly processed juices (most major brands) are absolutely not recommended as their sugar and preservative contents can be toxic and difficult to digest, and devoid of any real nutrition. Also avoid cow's milk, sodas, beer, wine or liquor. Green tea or black coffee is acceptable if your body is used to caffeine, but avoid adding dairy or sugar. You can add a bit of raw honey if you really need the sweetness. The important thing is to use the very highest quality liquid nutrition available with the highest quality supplementation to provide the most effective Intermittent Blasting experience.

5/2 Intermittent Blasting for Weight Loss

5/2 Intermittent Blasting is a very common strategy for most people seeking incremental weight loss over time. You Blast for a period of two days a week while eating normally the other five days. Your Blast days can be consecutive or nonconsecutive, as long as you have two Blast days within the week. Continue this regimen until you achieve your weight loss goal. Once you reach your ideal weight, Blast one day per week for optimal health and to maintain your ideal weight. This has proven to be very effective for steady, healthy weight loss of two to four pounds each week and is supported through both animal and human trials.

Every Other Day or Alternate Day Intermittent Blasting

If you want to lose weight more quickly, you can Blast every other day until you reach your desired weight. Using the Every-Other-Day approach you Blast three to four days per week rather than two, so weight loss will be more rapid. While on the surface, this may seem extreme, this method easily becomes second nature and achieves amazing results.

Dr. Krista Varady, a professor of nutrition at the University of Illinois, has conducted several successful human trials using this approach so the health benefits and weight loss are well established. Links to her published papers are located in the Appendix.

Lunch-to-Lunch (LTL) and Dinner-to-Dinner (DTD) Intermittent Blasting

Some people find it easier to Blast if they can eat solid food at least once every day. While we consider a "day" as getting up in the morning, being active during the day with breaks for sustenance, winding down in the evening and going to bed, our bodies are able to see things a bit differently. Our bodies will begin its restorative process anytime there is nothing left to digest. With Lunch-to-Lunch (LTL) or Dinner-to-Dinner (DTD) you can experience the benefits of Intermittent Blasting without going an entire day without eating solid food. Here's how it works:

If lunch is your main meal, a LTL Blast will work well for you. Your Intermittent Blasting starts after you finish lunch. After lunch, you enjoy your highly nutritious, easy-to-digest beverages every two-to-three hours or when you get hungry. You go to bed, get up the next morning and enjoy your beverages until lunchtime again. Then you have a full delicious meal for lunch. Your body has gone a full twenty-four hours without solid food while being Blasted with nutrition from the superfoods in your beverages, so the benefits and restorative process have begun. And the best thing is, you were asleep during a good part of it.

The LTL is great for anyone for whom lunch is the most important meal. Whether you're a business person who deals with working lunches and business luncheons, a stay-at-home parent who has social obligations at lunch, or anyone that is active on their job and needs that sustenance for the afternoon, you will find the LTL allows you to keep your obligations and be full of energy throughout the day. You can do this for as long as you want; whether it's one or two days or more. You'll amaze yourself at how easy it is.

For people who value dinner as their main meal of the day (especially those who often have dinner with family), the same concept can be applied. For DTD Blasting, begin your Blast immediately after dinner through bedtime, enjoying your nutritious beverage of choice if needed instead of snacking throughout the evening. The next day, continue with your beverages until dinner for a twenty-four-hour Intermittent Blast you will barely notice. Never miss dinners at home with family or meals out on the town with that special someone.

You can customize variations of these methods so Intermittent Blasting fits your lifestyle. Of course, you can try a Breakfast-to-Breakfast fast (BTB) if early morning meals get you going for the day. Extend your Intermittent Blasting from Lunch-to-Dinner (LTD) if you want to have a healthy lunch on Day One and carry your Blast all the way through dinner on Day Two. This will give you up to thirty hours of Intermittent Blasting and you never go an entire day without having solid food.

All of these methods of Intermittent Blasting will keep you on schedule, while still allowing your system to rest, rejuvenate and burn fat. These methods work well for maintaining weight, but depending on how many days you keep up the regimen, it can also be an excellent way to get down to an ideal weight in a more palatable manner. You never have a full day without having a meal so you can fulfill your social obligations without feeling a sense of deprivation.

Intermittent Blasting for Cleansing/Detoxing

For cleansing I recommend beginning with a two-day Blast as an introduction, followed by a three- to -five- day Blast once a month, or as desired. Some choose to extend their Blasts seven or even 10 days and beyond. Some prefer to Blast periodically one or two days per week while others prefer to Blast for a longer duration separated by more time. I have friends who Blast for five-to-seven days with every season change (four times a year). The choice is yours. However, I recommend you consult your healthcare practitioner before doing the Blast, especially if you choose to Blast longer than two days and certainly if you have any health condition.

Another consideration specifically for cleansing and detoxing is incorporating herbs or other ingredients to assist the body in the detoxification process. Juice or whole food ingredients can greatly enhance the cleansing process.

Digestive aids such as ginger, digestive enzymes, fermented foods and probiotics are great to support the digestive process while Intermittent Blasting, or while coming off a Blast. These foods support the digestive process and soothe the digestive tract.

Liver Support

Ingredients and foods such as beet or beet juice and/or milk thistle are great for detoxing the liver. Beet tablets were included in my first cleanse and I have since done several cleanses using fresh cold- pressed beet juice. One thing to remember when using a lot of beet either in supplement form or juice, your urine can become reddish in color. This is normal so don't freak out when you use the bathroom and see red.

Cleansing the Blood

Greens, greens and more greens. Greens such as spinach, kale, celery, broccoli, cucumbers, dandelion greens, spirulina and chlorella are rich in chlorophyll. Chlorophyll binds to environmental toxins such as heavy metals, herbicides, and pesticides and assists the body in ushering these toxins out of your system. I remember during my first cleanse I was instructed to take six spirulina tablets per day and they tasted terrible! Fortunately, now they come in capsule form and the tablets are coated so the taste isn't as prevalent.

Colon Detox

There are several schools of thought and many different products, foods and ingredients that can greatly assist the colon with the cleansing process. My favorite ingredients for pulling debris from the colon are psyllium husk powder, bentonite clay and activated charcoal. Each of these ingredients bind to toxins in the colon and help pull them out of your body. I used each of these on my very first cleanse and have continued to use them over the years.

Intermittent Blasting for Optimal Health

If you are already at your ideal weight, or once you achieve your ideal weight, you can optimize your health by Intermittent Blasting regularly. This allows you to maintain your ideal weight and supports many additional health benefits.

Intermittent fasting is known to provide the body with a wide range of health benefits for those seeking optimal health such as increasing testosterone, metabolism and HGH (Human Growth Hormone), helps the process of cellular repair by removing waste material from cells (autophagy), reduces insulin levels, oxidative stress and inflammation not to mention possible improvements in blood pressure, blood sugar, cholesterol and triglycerides. Intermittent fasting has even been implemented in improved brain function. Who couldn't use more brain power?

Recently studies have shown there are many additional benefits from intermittent fasting. These studies are listed in the Appendix for further research. Among the benefits of intermittent fasting that have been researched:

- Intermittent fasting can reduce your risk of type 2 diabetes
- Intermittent fasting may help prevent cancer
- Intermittent fasting may help prevent Alzheimer's Disease
- Intermittent fasting may extend your lifespan

Preparing for your Blast

For your very first Intermittent Blast, it's a good idea for you to select a day when you are going to be following your regular daily routine as much as possible. This will keep you focused and free of culinary surprises. Avoid parties and special functions if at all possible, because we all know how easy it is to mindlessly snack at social functions. Once you have Blasted a few times these distractions will become less difficult to navigate when you are Blasting. And of course, keep in mind that the beauty of Intermittent Blasting is that you can eat normally on days you are not Blasting which is most of the time.

But for now, pick a time when you will be mostly following your daily routine. Try to plan special activities during your typical mealtimes to take your mind off eating. Remember that the act of eating is sometimes more social than anything. Perhaps while you are on your Intermittent Blast you can run errands, start a personal project, or work on that novel you've always wanted to write. The important thing is to keep your mind busy and off the habit of eating. We often eat simply because we are bored.

Find Blast Buddies

One of the things that took me by surprise when this concept was growing organically with my co-workers and friends, was that people seemed to really enjoy doing an Intermittent Blast with a friend or group. They would encourage and support each other as well as provide distractions. Again, eating in our society is extremely social, so these groups served as a social substitute for dinner or lunch engagements. They would get together by twos and threes or more at a coffee shop for tea, or in each other's homes to watch movies or chat.

One of the interesting things that happened is that these groups would gather before their Blast for an evening out with food and drink. They consume a nice meal, discuss their strategies and toast their success. Some called these events "Blast-Off Dinners" or even "The Blast Supper" but it serves the function to officially launch the Blast for everyone so they were all on the same page from the start. So, I would highly recommend recruiting a Blast Buddy to join you on your journey to optimum health.

Ongoing Maintenance

Something that can be easily incorporated into your daily routine on non-Blast days is to begin each day with fresh squeezed vegetable and fruit juice or a smoothie. Have your breakfast as late in the morning as possible. This will give your body a great start with the highest quality nutrition without burdening your system with the difficult task of digesting. By delaying consumption of solid food each morning, you will give your body a longer window of opportunity to continue to rest and repair before you have a larger meal, which will put your body in a mode of digestion. The more time between your last meal of the day and the first meal of the following day the longer your body will have to rest and recuperate.

A Warning About Caffeine!

If you currently consume caffeine daily (coffee, tea or sodas) please consider continuing your caffeine consumption during your Intermittent Blast. Suddenly going without caffeine can cause you to experience a bad headache, nervousness or other unpleasant effects as a result caffeine withdrawal. This can be detrimental to your Blast experience. Switching to green tea over coffee or soda is recommended, or you can continue with coffee while trying to eliminate sugar, cream or other additives. Most people do not realize the amount of caffeine they are consuming on a day-to-day basis, so please be aware that headaches and other caffeine withdrawal symptoms are NOT a normal part of your Intermittent Blasting experience and can be easily alleviated with some green tea or coffee. The important thing is to NOT go "cold turkey" on your caffeine consumption.

Chapter 16: Intermittent Blasting!

One of the great things about Intermittent Blasting is its simplicity - no counting calories, no meal plans, no pills. As we've discussed previously in this book, there are many ways to do your Intermittent Blast: 5/2, Alternate Day, and LTL or DTD. However, one of the most effective and popular ways to Blast is for two consecutive days, which maximizes your benefits in both health and weight loss.

If you are going to do a consecutive two-day Intermittent Blast, there are a few things you should keep in mind. Your body has grown accustomed to non-stop availability of food 24/7, so there may be a period of adjustment for this kind of Blast. But remember, every time you Blast it gets easier. Soon, it will be incorporated into your life rather seamlessly.

Day 1

Begin your day by squeezing half a lemon in an eight-ounce glass of warm water on your Blast days. This is not required, but is recommended. Lemons are ideal to incorporate into any detoxification regimen and you are detoxifying to some degree when you Blast. Lemon is very cleansing to the liver, causing toxins to be dumped by stimulating its natural enzymes which helps keep skin even-toned and wrinkle-free. Lemons act to dissolve uric acid and other poisons, liquefy bile, and help to dissolve gallstones, calcium deposits, and kidney stones. Lemons increase peristalsis helping to eliminate waste. Lemons have powerful antibacterial properties; experiments have found the juice of lemons destroys the bacterial causes of malaria, cholera, diphtheria, typhoid and other deadly diseases. If you find that you enjoy the fresh lemon juice in the morning I would recommend you continue having it on a daily basis, even on your non-Blast days. This is a practice of many long-lived people and cultures worldwide -- one I've done for many years and something that I believe to be very beneficial.

Getting Through the Day

Have your drinks and/or mixers already prepared and know ahead of time which ones you are going to consume at what times throughout your day. For example, if you choose to have a vegetable juice like carrot or a V-8 type of drink you might enjoy that later in the day. If you are juicing, go ahead and prepare your juices in the morning or if you decide to purchase juices just know which ones you plan to have at what times. Remember we are avoiding hard-to-digest items, so whey protein powder and most complex carbs are off limits.

Have your first Blast drink thirty minutes to an hour after your lemon water and always remember to drink plenty of water in between drinks. After your first beverage, you will be amazed how quickly the feelings of hunger goes away and how alert and focused you will feel. Since your body isn't busy digesting, its energy is now helping you stay awake and alert. No more of the afternoon drowsiness most people experience on a daily basis. Plan on consuming six drinks for the whole day, but you can drink more or less depending on how you feel. Space them out about two-to-three hours apart.

You will probably begin to feel the first hunger pangs around two o'clock. Usually this is merely the result of the stomach adjusting to lack of contents. If you experience real hunger go ahead and have your next beverage. And please don't wait too long between servings. This can result in being overly hungry. If you feel hunger before two or three hours has elapsed go ahead and have another severing. Conversely, if you do not feel hungry and it's been two or three hours since your last serving go ahead and consume your next beverage anyway, so you don't get hungry.

The first day is the most difficult for most people. If this is the case with you, just power through it; it gets easier, I promise.

In the late afternoon and early evening, you will probably be in the habit of thinking about what's for dinner. Try to keep your mind occupied with other things – go to a movie, run errands or do a slow, simple workout such as tai chi, yoga or take a leisurely walk.

In the evening, try to relax or invite your Blast Buddies over for game night or just to chat about how things are going. Most people are going strong and feel energized when they go to bed, but end up sleeping soundly and through the night.

Tips from Experienced Intermittent Blasters

"If you are the family chef, consider cooking all family meals in advance of your start day."

"Avoid the kitchen as much as possible."

"Don't watch TV with commercials."

"Definitely don't watch your favorites on the Food Network or Cooking channels."

"Avoid using citrus juices as they can be harsh on the stomach."

Day 2

Again, begin the day with fresh lemon juice and warm water. You may be surprised how little hunger you feel. But if you are hungry, your first serving should take care of it. Today will be a bit different as your body really gets into cleansing mode and detoxification. These symptoms will vary and should be mild. However, by mid-day you might feel a slight headache or light-headed. This is a normal part of the cleansing process and should not be confused with "starvation."

Our society trains us to think that if we feel the slightest bit of discomfort, it's a bad thing. But in this case, it is a very good thing and should not be of concern.

Take it easy, drink plenty of water and again consume an extra beverage if you feel the need. And be sure to call your Blast Buddies and see how they are doing. By evening you should be feeling fine. Again, sleeping tonight should be sounder than ever and you will wake up the next day feeling refreshed and full of energy.

Coming Off Your Intermittent Blast

When doing a Blast of two or more days it is important to slowly incorporate solid foods and foods that are more difficult to digest. On your first day of eating solid foods following your Blast it is highly recommended to start with foods that are very easy on your digestive tract. As good as it may sound you wouldn't want to have foods such as pizza, burger and fries or a steak.

After giving your digestive system a rest, when you begin to introduce solid foods it's best to start with something like a fruit and vegetable smoothie, steamed vegetables or vegetable soup.

I have come to enjoy looking forward to a special meal before cleansing and afterward. For my last meal leading up to an Intermittent Blast I usually have a nice dinner at a restaurant that I don't frequent very often - something a little special. And for the first meal following my Blast, I enjoy the whole process of going and picking out my vegetables for my soup and getting up in the morning and making a big pot that I end up eating over the next several days. I'm sure you will have your own preferences, but the main thing to remember is to be sure to not introduce foods that are difficult to digest too quickly.

Once you've completed your Blast, you will be feeling healthier, happier and most certainly lighter! Treat yourself to something special, go to a movie, get a massage...do something for YOU that you normally don't do. Pampering and indulging yourself a bit is a great reward – you've earned it!

I would highly recommend the companion book, *Intermittent Blasting Recipes,* which has numerous excellent recipes for juices, smoothies and soups. There are recipes to use during your Intermittent Blast, coming off your Intermittent Blast and for daily use.

Simple Smoothie

This is a smoothie I have been making for years. I vary it slightly depending on what's in season but the base stays the same. Always use fresh, local, organic produce when possible.

- 1 cup blueberries
- ½ cup mango
- ½ avocado
- 1 small or ½ large apple
- 1 handful spinach
- Just enough water to mix

Blend until smooth.

Additions for variety:

- Peaches or strawberries
- For veggies, add raw or steamed carrots, cauliflower or a hand full of greens of your choice
- For protein, add a raw egg or protein from brown rice, hemp, pea or pumpkinseed
- For fat/fiber, add soaked flax seeds or coconut butter
- Substitute carrot juice for water

Other Smoothie Recipes

Banana Berry Fruit Smoothie

- 1 banana
- 6 strawberries
- Flax seed milk or almond milk
- Handful of spinach
- 1 tablespoon cinnamon

Lemon Green Smoothie

- 1 avocado
- A few slices apple
- 1 cucumber
- 2 cups spinach
- 2 large collard greens leaves
- 2 leaves black kale
- Juice of 3 lemons
- 1-1/2 cups water

Fruit and Salad smoothie with mint

- 1/2 cup water
- 1 apple, cut in pieces
- 1 cup white grapes
- 1/3 cucumber, skinned and cut in large pieces
- 2 lettuce leaves
- 1/2 stick celery, cut in pieces
- 1 tablespoon fresh mint leaves

Simple Veggie Soup

- 2 cloves garlic, peeled and minced
- 1 small onion, peeled and diced
- 1/4 green bell pepper, diced
- 1/4 red bell pepper, diced
- 3 medium carrots, diced
- 1/2 cup Brussels sprouts
- 4 medium potatoes, diced
- 1/4 cup green peas
- 1/4 cup black-eyed peas
- 1/4 cup kidney beans
- 1/4 cup lentils
- 2 cups tomato juice

- 32 ounces bone broth, or organic vegetable broth (Imagine or Pacific, for example)
- Salt, pepper and spices of choice, to taste

If you are using un-prepped (raw) beans, lentils, and peas, they should be soaked in water overnight. Start by sweating the onion, garlic, and peppers in a heavy cast-iron skillet with coconut oil, olive oil, or red palm oil until soft. Transfer to a large pot filled with a couple of cups of tomato juice and thirty-two ounces of bone broth, or organic vegetable broth (Imagine, 365, or Pacific, for example). Cook on medium to high heat until the soup reaches a boil and lower heat to medium-low. After prepping the additional ingredients (washing all produce thoroughly, and dicing the potatoes and carrots), add everything to the pot except the potatoes. Cook on medium-low heat for thirty to forty minutes, then add the potatoes. Continue to cook an additional twenty minutes until potatoes are soft throughout. Take the pot off the heat and serve.

Chapter 17: Frequently Asked Questions

Below you will find some of the most frequently asked questions that may arise as you consider doing your first Intermittent Blast. Please read this section thoroughly to find the answers to some things that might be on your mind. Some of these may seem obvious or basic, but they are all worth reviewing before your first Blast.

Why should I Blast?

Simply put, Intermittent Blasting allows you to lose weight quickly in the healthiest way possible. Intermittent Blasting provides your digestive system time to rest, allowing your body to use energy for cleansing, rejuvenating and burning fat. You will likely experience an increase in energy, mental clarity, relaxation and joy...and you are sure to lose unwanted pounds.

When is a good time to plan my Intermittent Blast?

You can Blast anytime, even while maintaining your usual daily activities. It is a good idea to schedule your first Blast when you're not obligated to attend business or family functions based around meals.

How often should I Blast?

We recommend Intermittent Blasting for two days a week until you reach your weight loss goal and then once or twice a week as needed to maintain your ideal weight. Consider a Blast at the first sign of a cold or following any sort of overindulging; like on holidays, sporting events and other special times. Make it a habit, and your body will thank you for it.

How many calories will I consume per day during my Blast?

Around 500 - 700 calories a day, based on consuming six servings at around one hundred calories each. Please keep in mind all calories are not equal. Empty calories from a hamburger and fries are not the same as calories from organic fruits and vegetables. Think nutritional content, not calorie content.

If I feel hungry, can I eat solid food during my Intermittent Blast?

Your brain is used to you eating all the time, so it is natural for you to feel hungry. But when you think about it, you might find that feeling of hunger is more a "phantom" of memory than actual hunger. We eat to be social and we eat when we're bored, but for the most part true "hunger" comes about only in extreme circumstances. If you become hungry in between servings, drink a glass of water to help suppress your appetite.

Should I drink water during my Intermittent Blast?

YES! Be sure to drink plenty of water throughout the day. Drinking water can serve as a natural appetite-suppressant by providing a filling sensation in the stomach. Additionally, during your Intermittent Blast your body will be unloading a variety of toxins into your bloodstream and colon. It is very important to help the body flush the toxins by drinking plenty of water.

Can I drink coffee while on my Intermittent Blast?

If you usually consume caffeine, make sure to drink a cup of coffee or green tea to avoid a possible headache from caffeine withdrawal. However, avoid adding cream, sugar or artificial sweeteners to lessen your caloric intake.

Can I take protein powder on my Intermittent Blast?

Protein (especially animal protein) takes longer to digest which does not allow for proper rest and rejuvenation of the digestive system. If you feel the need to supplement protein (perhaps due to a medical condition), we recommend organic pea, brown rice or hemp protein.

Can I exercise on my Intermittent Blast?

You may want to take it easy on your first Intermittent Blast but all types of exercise routines are encouraged. There is a common misperception that eating is necessary to supply "energy" to the working body which is just not true. The liver supplies energy via gluconeogenesis. During longer fasting periods, the muscles are also able to use fatty acids directly for energy. As your adrenaline levels will be higher, Intermittent Blasting is an ideal time to exercise. Pay attention to what your body is telling you and adjust your exercise accordingly while on your Intermittent Blast.

Will I experience any side effects on my Intermittent Blast?

During your Intermittent Blast, the body is burning stored fat, as well as cleaning out all the accumulated toxins that have built up over time—all the while rebuilding cells with new material. Intermittent Blasting is specifically designed to allow for gradual elimination and to keep your detoxification symptoms to a minimum. However, you may experience some slight symptoms such as headaches, fatigue or rash depending on your current level of toxicity.

What should I eat when I finish my Intermittent Blast?

Most people find they do not have much of an appetite coming off their Blast. Consuming small simple meals, the first day after your Intermittent Blast is highly recommended.

Can I Blast while pregnant or nursing?

Intermittent Blasting is not recommended for pregnant or nursing mothers. Pregnant women should not restrict calories as expectant mothers need maximum nutrition. Furthermore, the toxins released into the bloodstream during an Intermittent Blast can be harmful to growing babies.

Are there benefits to a one-day Intermittent Blast?

Absolutely! How would you feel if you never had a day off? The benefits of a one-day Intermittent Blast are amazing! Fasting has been used for centuries as a strategy to strengthen the immune system and sharpen mental clarity.

If a two-day Intermittent Blast helps, how about three to five days or longer?

The length of your Intermittent Blast is a personal decision. We recommend two days per week for healthy weight loss as many of the clinical trials on intermittent fasting are based on that timeframe.

Each additional day you add is more time for your body to experience the benefits of fat burning and cleansing.

Can I Use Intermittent Blasting if I have diabetes?

With any existing medical condition, such as diabetes, it is highly recommended to consult your physician. Most juices and smoothies recommended for Intermittent Blasting contains a very balanced mixture of carbohydrates, protein, healthy fat and fiber with no added sugars. However, greatly reducing calories can cause a deviation in insulin, so caution is warranted for diabetics. Diabetics may wish to begin Blasting by skipping only one meal, then gradually add additional time after they monitor the effect Intermittent Blasting has on their individual system.

Again, please check with your physician because blood sugar must be monitored very closely especially if you are on medication.

Can I try Intermittent Blasting if I am lactose or gluten intolerant?

Certainly! There are no animal products or gluten contained in any of the suggested Intermittent Blasting juice or smoothie recipes.

Can my child use Intermittent Blasting?

Ideally, it is best to avoid calorie restriction while children are growing. However, with childhood obesity at an all-time high, it can be considered on a case-by-case basis. It is recommended that you consult with your child's physician.

Can I have seltzer or sparkling water? How about sodas or other drinks?

Seltzer or sparkling water is not ideal because it will contribute gas to your system. However, it's not a bad option if it will keep you from drinking other beverages. Drinking sodas is not recommended on your Intermittent Blast. Sodas are filled with sugar and other undesirable chemicals and are very acidifying. Try to drink water with lemon or herbal or green tea instead.

Will I get light-headed if I'm not eating solid food?

It's possible that a mild light-headedness or headache could occur at some point during your Intermittent Blast. However, many people find that they do not experience this at all. All the energy usually taken up by the digestive process will be available for restoration and rejuvenation. Usually one's mind becomes clearer and one's ability to solve problems increases.

Will I burn muscle while on my Intermittent Blast?

On your Intermittent Blast the body first breaks down glycogen into glucose for energy. After that, the body increases fat breakdown to provide energy. Therefore, the body will not burn muscle during your Intermittent Blast.

I haven't gone to the bathroom at all, and I'm on day two. Is that normal?

Reduced input means reduced output. This is completely normal.

Chapter 18: Intermittent Blasting for Life

ABB - "Always Be Blasting"

There's a strategy in sales abbreviated as ABC, which stands for "Always Be Closing." Considering 95 percent of Americans are deficient in nutrition and we are experiencing epidemic rates of chronic disease, I believe we should adopt a strategy of ABB; "Always Be Blasting." We need to blast our bodies with high-quality nutrition at every opportunity. Anytime we eat, we have a choice of what we put into our bodies: a choice of putting in junk food with little or no nutritional value, or consuming superfoods and blasting our bodies with quality nutrients. Keeping this in mind will help you consume the very best nutrition available every time you eat, whether you are on a Blast or not.

Living a Healthy Life

Intermittent Blasting is a great tool for managing weight and restoring health. As we have discussed throughout this book, our health in the modern world is suffering. We as a people are suffering. Chronic disease is rampant and has become an expected and accepted part of life. Intermittent Blasting is a way people living in a modern society can lose weight and improve their health. But overall, we need to rethink our lifestyle from a larger perspective. One that combines science, modernization and food processing in healthier ways, not just profitable and convenient ones. Because when we, as a society, are unhealthy we all suffer, both health-wise and economically.

A Healthy Diet in A Nutshell

Food Groups to Include:

- Vegetables and salads: At least three servings of vegetables at lunch and three at supper—including garlic and onions and dark green leafy vegetables (e.g., broccoli, spinach, bell peppers, zucchini, lettuce, carrots, cucumber, celery, celeriac, fennel, sweet potatoes, green beans, green peas, etc.).
- Fruit: Daily - One to three pieces.
- Grains: If you choose to include grains, choose whole grains in moderate quantities instead of refined grains. Oats, millet, rye, barley, brown rice, red rice, quinoa, buckwheat, amaranth, and whole wheat.
- Vegetable proteins: Daily or most days - nuts, beans, lentils, miso, seeds, flax seeds, chia seeds, and sprouted seeds.

- Animal proteins: In small quantities - eggs, fish from an unpolluted source, live plain yogurt, organic beef, organic cheese from goat's or sheep's milk. In small to moderate quantities—lean organic poultry.
- Monounsaturated fats: Daily or most days - from unheated extra virgin olive oil, avocados, nuts; if cooking with olive oil, keep the heat low and cooking time short.
- Omega 3 essential fatty acids: Daily - oily fish, ground flax seed, chia seed, walnuts, supplements.
- Omega 6 essential fatty acids: Daily - nuts and seeds, some oils, ground flax seed, chia seed, avocado.
- Fermented foods: Small amounts daily or several times per week - live plain yogurt, kefir, sauerkraut, miso, tempeh and traditionally marinated vegetables.
- Water: Several glasses daily, sipped throughout the day. At least ½ ounce per pound of bodyweight.
- Green tea, herb tea: Daily.
- Red wine: Stick to small amounts of organic red wine, with a meal, and try not to drink every day - if you drink alcohol, red wine has the most health advantages and the least disadvantages.
- Fiber: Daily, both soluble and insoluble, sourced in your fruits, vegetables, nuts, seeds, and grains.

Food groups to exclude/restrict:
- Refined sugar
- Refined carbs (white flour, white rice)
- Alcohol
- Caffeine
- Trans fats from processed foods
- Damaged fats from cooking oils
- Non-organic dairy products

Cooking Tips

- Use fresh, local, organic produce when possible.
- Use meat as a flavoring for a dish, rather than making it the "star" of the meal.
- Use organic pasture-raised, grass-fed meat when possible.
- Use herbs and spices to flavor recipes, rather than lots of refined salt. Experiment with some that you haven't used before—the internet is a great resource for finding out how to use new herbs & spices. Use Celtic Sea Salt, Himalayan Pink or Real Salt when using salt.
- Use filtered water when a recipe calls for water.
- Boiling or poaching is best to preserve the nutrients in eggs; second-best is scrambled.
- Remember not to overcook vegetables. Lightly steaming, gently roasting, or just eating raw are preferred methods.
- Toss together different colors of vegetables to arouse your eyes and taste buds.
- Use first cold-pressed olive oil in salads and when drizzling over other foods.
- Use coconut oil when cooking at higher heat.
- Steam or slow-roast vegetables. Or eat them raw to preserve vitamins, minerals, and enzymes.
- Avoid burning or charring meat. This can create pro-aging free radicals and carcinogenic heterocyclic aromatic amines (HAAs). Grill with indirect heat only.
- Use fresh herbs, garlic, lemon, and spices such as turmeric liberally in your food preparation for flavor.
- Try to consume foods grown and prepared locally to ensure they are as fresh as possible.
- Avoid frying. It damages oils and can make them unhealthy.
- If pan-searing or frying, use oils with a very high smoke point, such as coconut (preferred), red palm or avocado

oils. These oils are more stable at higher temperatures than corn or olive oil.

- Use meat and dairy products as a condiment to flavor vegetable dishes, rather than using them as the main feature of your dishes.

Shopping Tips

- Read labels.
- When grocery shopping, choose locally- grown produce and meats - no chemicals, processing, or preservatives.
- Keep to the perimeter of the grocery store, where the fresh produce tends to be. Avoid the interior aisles, where the chips and other junk foods tend to be.
- On the interior aisles, avoid the UFOs - unidentified food objects. You'll know them when you see ingredients that are artificial, unrecognizable and unpronounceable.
- When purchasing fruits and vegetables, always look for labels such as Local, Organic, and No GMO (genetically modified organisms).
- If you can't find fresh produce, your second choice should be frozen fruits and vegetables. Canned foods are lower in nutrients.
- Look for free-range, organic beef and poultry products. Levels of harmful chemicals should be much lower than in the products of industrial-farmed animals.
- Choose deep-water, wild-caught ocean fish, which is likely to have lower levels of mercury, PCBs, dioxin, and other toxic, cancer-causing chemicals. Avoid farm-raised fish. Wild-caught Alaskan salmon is preferred.
- Avoid having tuna more than twice per month. It can be high in mercury. Choose tuna caught by the pole-and-line method.

- When buying breads, choose one hundred percent whole grain rather than white breads made with refined flours. Avoid high-calorie pastries altogether.
- Avoid high-sugar snacks. Choose whole-grain crackers or baked snacks.
- Try to buy nuts in their shells, since the oils in pre-shelled nuts go rancid quickly. Children love cracking the shells open, so it's a great way to eat nuts.
- Choose water, fresh juice, herbal tea, and organic, fair-trade coffee over sugary soft drinks and avoid diet soft drinks and other diet beverages that contain harmful chemicals.
- "Sugar-free" on the label only refers to sucrose or table sugar. Other sugars to watch for are fructose, maltose, lactose, glucose, dextrose, corn-syrup solids, corn sweeteners, and hydrolyzed corn starch.
- Look for products with healthier sweeteners, such as fruit, stevia, evaporated cane juice, or agave. Try sweetening your coffee and tea with raw honey instead of table sugar.
- Use Celtic Sea Salt, Himalayan Pink salt or Real Salt brand salt rather than refined table salt, as they are unrefined and contain beneficial minerals.
- When buying soaps, lotions, cleaners, and detergents, look for unscented products. Items with fragrances may contain potentially harmful chemicals.
- Avoid antibacterial soaps with the chemicals triclosan and triclocarban. They're thought to affect reproductive hormones as well as the nervous system and might contribute to the evolution of antibiotic-resistant superbugs.

APPENDICES - FURTHER STUDY

Appendix A: Juicing

I am a huge advocate of juicing and I encourage everyone to juice at home when possible. However, juicing is time consuming, and in reality, most people simply can't spare time from their busy schedules to juice on a frequent basis. Fortunately, there has been a recent surge in companies providing fresh, organic, cold- pressed juice. I say fortunately, because years ago when I started juicing there were no companies selling fresh, organic juice; I had to make it myself. Now there are many viable options; it's just a matter of logistics. If you live in a major metropolitan area like New York City or Los Angeles you will have no trouble finding a local company happy to supply you with fresh, organic, cold- pressed beverages. However, if you live outside the larger cities, finding a local company providing this service may prove to be more difficult, and you may have to consider purchasing from a vendor online. Fresh, organic, cold- pressed vegetable and fruit juice is basically gourmet liquid nutrition so it does not come cheap. Even if you do it yourself it is quite expensive. Keep in mind however, these beverages are extremely high quality and if you are on the Blast you will likely save money as you are not purchasing your usual meals.

Purchasing fresh, organic, cold pressed juice

To locate companies providing these beverages you can simply conduct an internet search using your local zip code along with "organic cold press juice." Again, these beverages are much more expensive than ordinary juice but they are extremely high quality and I've found that the savings achieved by juicing yourself isn't very significant.

Juice with your own juicer

To make your own cold pressed or slow pressed juice you will need a juicer or a combination of two separate machines. The type of juicer you will want to purchase is either a "cold press" or "slow press" juicer. These juice extraction methods are far superior to a centrifugal style juicer. Cold press or slow press methods allows for a much higher integrity of nutrients as no heat is used in the process. Almost all the pulp is pressed out which means less oxygen, which in turn gives a better tasting, more nutritionally dense juice. Compared to the centrifugal juicing process these juices are much higher in nutrition. In fact, it is estimated that cold pressed juice contains three to five times more vitamins and minerals than fresh juice from a centrifugal juicer.

The gold standard of cold press juicers is the Norwalk and comes with a price of $2,500.00. A more economical way to produce fresh cold pressed juice is to purchase a grinder and a juice press. The grinder will cost around $300-$500 and the press is an additional $400. A simpler option is to purchase a slow juicer (which are known to produce similar quality juice as cold press juicers) and there are many options on the market. Some do a better job juicing harder produce such as beets and carrots while others do a better job with leafy greens, so there really is no single "best juicer." All things considered, I recommend the Hurom Slow Juicer or the Omega Vert which are identical units. These juicers are practicable, very efficient and can be purchased for around three hundred dollars.

Juice recipes

Juice recipes for optimizing nutrient intake and detoxification value on the Blast. When possible always use fresh, locally grown, organic produce.

A Simple, Green Juice: Apple, Celery, Cucumber, Kale, Lemon

- 1 cucumber
- 1 bunch of kale
- 4 celery stalks
- 1/2 lemon including skin
- 2 apples: Granny smith, gala or golden delicious if possible.

Wash all produce thoroughly. Cut the cucumber and apples into pieces small enough to fit into the juicer and cut the lemon in half. Juice the cucumber, kale, celery, lemon, and apples. Serve. Makes about 2 glasses of green juice.

This basic green beverage is packed with vitamins, minerals (especially calcium), enzymes, chlorophyll, protein, electrolytes, and phytonutrients. This drink is amazing for energy, muscle recovery and detoxification and is extremely alkalizing. Green vegetables in particular are extremely alkalizing and packed with chlorophyll, protein, enzymes, electrolytes, calcium and phytonutrients, which are great for energy, muscle recovery and detoxification of organs.

Liver cleanse: Beet, apple, carrot

- 1 large or 2 small apples
- 1 large or 2 small beets
- 3 large or 4 medium carrots

Wash all produce thoroughly. Cut the apples, beet and carrots into pieces small enough to fit into the juicer. Juice and serve. Makes about 2 glasses of juice.

This particular combination of fresh juices is terrific for cleansing the liver, lowers inflammation, aids blood circulation and is packed with potassium, magnesium, phosphorus, iron, vitamins A, B & C, beta-carotene, beta-cyanine, folic acid, and biotin. This juice has

144

powers of antimicrobial, antiviral, anti-aging, anti-inflammatory and antioxidants that help the body fight free radicals.

LemonAid: Apple, lemon

- 4 apples
- 1/4 lemon including skin

Wash all produce thoroughly. Cut the apples into pieces small enough to fit into the juicer and cut ¼ lemon. Juice and serve. Makes about 2 glasses.

This LemonAid is simple, delicious and very nutritious. A great source of antioxidants, flavonoids, electrolytes, is anti-inflammatory, antibacterial and cleanses the blood. This drink will help cleanse the liver and gallbladder, increase energy, and is very alkalizing.

Other Juice Options

In absence of organic, cold pressed juice you can substitute the juice of your choice as long as you select the highest quality organic juice available. Keep the sugar content low so as not to spike your blood sugar. Remember, the more sugar you consume, the less effective your Blast will be.

Benefits of various produce used in juicing

Apples

Apples are known to cleanse the gallbladder and liver. High in Malic acid which is said to play an important role in creating adenosine triphosphate (ATP). ATP is the body's primary source of energy at the cellular level. Apples also contain the potent detoxifying enzyme bromelain, which has cleansing, anti-inflammatory properties and cleanses the blood.

Beets

Beets are a wonderful tonic for the liver, work as a cleanser for the blood stream and are supportive of the heart and other circulatory systems in the body. Beets contain high amounts of boron, which is vital to the production of human sex hormones. Beets are filled with potassium, magnesium, phosphorus, iron; vitamins A, B, & C; beta-carotene, beta-cyanine; and folic acid. Beets contain betaine which is used in certain treatments of depression and also contains tryptophan, which relaxes the mind and creates a sense of well-being, similar to chocolate. Beets also contain folic acid which is necessary for the production of new cells. Beets contain the betalains betanin and vulgaxanthin. Both provide anti-inflammatory, antioxidant and detoxification support.

Carrots

Carrot juice is a great source of beta-carotene which is good for the eyes but also necessary for a shiny, well-moisturized hair and scalp. Carrots are packed with vitamins, minerals, and biotin, as well as powerful antioxidants, and also possess antimicrobial, antiviral, and anti-inflammatory properties, and aid blood circulation. Carrots are rich in vitamin A which protect us from sun damage. Carrots have strong cleansing properties that are effective in detoxifying the liver, and very effective for treating acne that is caused by toxins from the blood. The vitamin A and other nutrients contained in carrots nourish the skin, prevent dry skin and other skin blemishes. Carrots contain a lot of beta-carotene, which serves as an antioxidant that helps the body to fight against free radicals. It also helps slow down the aging of cells and various negative effects associated with aging. Carrots are also high in potassium, an essential electrolyte necessary for cell function.

Celery

A true superfood, the simple celery plant provides an amazing number of important nutrients assisting many functions in the body.

Celery is very alkalizing, highly nutritious and is one of the most hydrating foods on the planet. The polyacetylene in celery is a powerful anti-inflammatory and the potassium and sodium in celery juice are powerful body fluid regulators that stimulate urine production to help rid the body of excess fluid. Celery contains important concentrations of plant hormones and the very special essential oils that give celery its characteristic smell. These oils help to regulate the nervous system, and have a calming effect on the nervous system, making it beneficial for insomniacs. Its high magnesium levels help people to relax into a soothing and restful sleep. Celery juice is an amazing eliminator of toxins from the body, which aids in the breaking down and elimination of urinary and gall bladder stones.

Cucumber

Cucumber is super hydrating and charged with active enzymes, B vitamins, antioxidants, and electrolytes. Cucumber is full of beautifying silica, as well as caffeic acid, which has anti-inflammatory properties. Cucumber is extremely hydrating and is beneficial for the skin. Cucumbers have most of the vitamins the body needs in a single day. Due to its low calorie and high water content, cucumber is an ideal food for people who are looking for weight loss. The high structured water content in cucumbers is very effective in ridding the body of toxins from the digestive system and is very alkalizing.

Lemons

Lemons are rich in the free-radical fighting antioxidant vitamin C, and flavonoids which help to neutralize free radicals linked to aging and most disease. Lemons improve blood flow and reduce inflammation. Though acidic to the taste, lemons are very alkalizing in the body. Lemons are a good source of electrolytes, such as potassium, calcium and magnesium. Your liver loves lemons. Lemon is cleansing to the liver, causing toxins to be dumped by stimulating its natural enzymes, which helps keep skin even-toned and wrinkle-free. Lemons are a dissolvent of uric acid and other poisons, liquefies bile, help dissolve gallstones, calcium deposits, and kidney stones. Lemons increase peristalsis, helping to eliminate waste. Lemons have powerful antibacterial properties; experiments have found the juice of lemons destroys the bacteria of malaria, cholera, diphtheria, typhoid and other deadly diseases.

Kale

One of the healthiest vegetables on the planet, kale is in the brassica family which includes cruciferous vegetables such as cabbage, collards, broccoli, and Brussels sprouts. Kale is a nutritional powerhouse packed with calcium, vitamin B6, magnesium, vitamin A, vitamin C, and vitamin K. It is also a good source of the minerals copper, potassium, iron, manganese, and phosphorus. Kale is also rich in eye-health promoting lutein and zeaxanthin. Per calorie, kale has more calcium than milk, which helps keep bones strong. Kale has more iron than beef, making it a great food for vegans and vegetarians. The vitamin A in kale is great for vision, skin and nails. Kale is high in antioxidants such as carotenoids and flavonoids, is anti-inflammatory and extremely alkalizing. Amazingly, kale also has a healthy balance of omega-3 and omega-6 fatty acids.

Parsley

Parsley is much more than a decorative item placed on your plate to be discarded. Parsley is super rich with antioxidants including luteolin, a flavonoid that eradicates free radicals in the body that cause oxidative stress in cells. Luteolin also promotes carbohydrate metabolism and is anti-inflammatory. Parsley is especially high in two powerful antioxidants, vitamins C and A which serve to strengthen the body's immune system. Vitamin C is necessary for collagen production, the main structural protein found in connective tissue. This essential nutrient will not only accelerate the body's ability to repair wounds, but also maintain healthy bones and teeth.

Vitamin A fortifies the entry points into the human body, such as mucous membranes, the lining of the eyes, and the respiratory, urinary and intestinal tracts. Furthermore, white blood cells rely on vitamin A to fight infection in the body. Parsley is also a great source of vitamin B12, vitamin K, beta carotene, folic acid and iron. Parsley (as are greens in general) is a power-plant of chlorophyll, which is anti-bacterial and extremely alkalizing. Chlorophyll found in parsley is a good cure for bad breath. It also helps flush out excess fluid from the body which supports kidney function.

Spinach

Spinach is an excellent source of vitamin K, vitamin A, magnesium, folate, manganese, iron, calcium, vitamin C, vitamin B2, potassium, vitamin B6 and a host of trace minerals. It's a very good source of protein, phosphorus, vitamin E, zinc, beta-carotene, and copper. Plus, it's a good source of selenium, niacin, and omega-3 fatty acids. The high amount of vitamin A in spinach promotes healthy skin by allowing for proper moisture retention in the epidermis, thus fighting psoriasis, keratinization, acne and even wrinkles. Vitamin K in spinach promotes the synthesis of osteocalcin, the protein that is essential for maintaining the strength and density of our bones. It also contributes greatly to a healthy nervous system and brain function, by providing an essential part for the synthesis of sphingolipids, the crucial fat that makes up the myelin sheath around our nerves. Spinach is loaded with flavonoids which act as antioxidants, protecting the body from free radicals. DNA damage and mutations in colon cells may be prevented by the folate that's present in spinach. In comparison to red meat, spinach provides a lot less calories, and is an excellent source of iron. Because iron is a component of hemoglobin, which carries oxygen to all body cells, it's needed for energy. Spinach is also anti-Inflammatory and very alkalizing.

Appendix B: Further Research into Benefits of Intermittent Fasting

In addition to the many scientific studies and articles I have cited in the main part of this book, there are dozens more that support the concepts of intermittent fasting and its positive effects on our health. I present here my favorite articles and studies for you to continue to research this should you be the kind of person who enjoys digging deeper into the science. There are some truly remarkable findings here and I hope you take the time to read some of this material.

General Articles

Krista Varady weighs in on how to drop pounds

https://news.uic.edu/krista-varady-weighs-in-on-how-to-drop-pounds-fast

Lean and Lovin' it: British author shares her take on Intermittent Blasting

http://www.dailyherald.com/article/20131008/entlife/710089950/

Experiments with Intermittent Fasting

http://www.precisionnutrition.com/intermittent-fasting

Intermittent Fasting and high intensity fitness boost HGH

http://www.naturalnews.com/034704_intermittent_fasting_fitness_HGH.htm

Intermittent Fasting – Getting Younger Every Day!

http://www.sunwarrior.com/blog/weight-loss/intermittent-fasting-getting-younger-every-day

Intermittent Fasting: the next big weight loss fad

http://www.cmaj.ca/content/early/2013/03/25/cmaj.109-4437

Experiments with Intermittent Fasting - By Dr. John M. Bernrdi with Dr. Krista Scott-Dixon and Nate Green

http://www.precisionnutrition.com/intermittent-fasting

Does Intermittent Fasting Work? - Intermittent Fasting is a powerful tool. This is why.

http://health.usnews.com/health-news/blogs/eat-run/2013/11/01/does-intermittent-fasting-work

Short Fasts for Weight Loss vs. Traditional Diets - How Drastic Reduction of Calories for Limited Periods of Time Compares to Other Plans

http://online.wsj.com/news/articles/SB10001424052702304854804579234140222181848

Study Shows Why It's Hard to Keep Weight Off

http://www.nytimes.com/2011/10/27/health/biological-changes-thwart-weight-loss-efforts-study-finds.html

BBC News January 2, 2013 - Diet doctor urges Intermittent Fasting

http://www.bbc.com/news/health-20890613

7 Ways That Intermittent Fasting Boosts Your Metabolism to Burn Fat

http://www.livestrong.com/article/534073-7-ways-that-intermittent-fasting-energizes-your-metabolism-to-burn-fat/

Eat Stop Eat – The Shocking Truth that Makes Weight Loss Simple Again

This ebook by Brad Pilon is a great resource on intermittent fasting.

> ✉ http://eatstopeat.com/

7 Ways Fasting Can Rev Up Your Fat Burning Furnace

One of my personal favorite articles by Brad Pilon, author of *Eat Stop Eat*.

> ✉ http://jasonferruggia.com/7-ways-fasting-fat-burning-furnace/

The Juice-Bar Brawl

> ✉ http://www.nytimes.com/2013/04/17/dining/the-rush-toward-cold-pressed-juices.html

Nerd Fitness - The Beginner's Guide to Intermittent Fasting

> ✉ http://www.nerdfitness.com/blog/2013/08/06/a-beginners-guide-to-intermittent-fasting/

The Lean Gains Guide - Intermittent Fasting and Lean gains

> ✉ http://www.leangains.com/2010/04/leangains-guide.html

The Extreme Muscle Building Secrets of UFC Fighters

> ✉ http://www.fourhourworkweek.com/blog/2013/05/11/how-to-gain-20-pounds-in-28-days-the-extreme-muscle-building-secrets-of-ufc-fighters/

Fasting may protect against disease; some say it may even be good for the brain

> 📄 http://www.washingtonpost.com/national/health-science/fasting-may-protect-against-disease-some-say-it-may-even-be-good-for-the-brain/2012/12/24/6e521ee8-3588-11e2-bb9b-288a310849ee_story.html

Scientific Studies

Harvard study shows how intermittent fasting and manipulating mitochondrial networks may increase lifespan

> 📄 https://news.harvard.edu/gazette/story/2017/11/intermittent-fasting-may-be-center-of-increasing-lifespan/

Fasting enhances growth hormone secretion and amplifies the complex rhythms of growth hormone secretion in man.

> 📄 https://www.ncbi.nlm.nih.gov/pmc/articles/PMC329619/

Growth hormone and sex steroid administration in healthy aged women and men: a randomized controlled trial.

> 📄 https://www.ncbi.nlm.nih.gov/pubmed/12425705

Fasting enhances growth hormone secretion and amplifies the complex rhythms of growth hormone secretion in man.

> 📄 https://www.ncbi.nlm.nih.gov/pubmed/3127426

Augmented growth hormone (GH) secretory burst frequency and amplitude mediate enhanced GH secretion during a two-day fast in normal men.

https://www.ncbi.nlm.nih.gov/pubmed/1548337

The effect of intermittent energy and carbohydrate restriction v. daily energy restriction on weight loss and metabolic disease risk markers in overweight women.

http://www.ncbi.nlm.nih.gov/pubmed/23591120

"In the short term, IECR is superior to DER with respect to improved insulin sensitivity and body fat reduction. Longer-term studies into the safety and effectiveness of IECR diets are warranted."

Alternate day calorie restriction (ADCR) improves clinical findings and reduces markers of oxidative stress and inflammation in overweight adults with moderate asthma

http://www.sciencedirect.com/science/article/pii/S089158490600801X

Although obesity is a risk factor for asthma and weight loss can improve symptoms, many patients do not adhere to low calorie diets and the impact of dietary restriction on the disease process is unknown. A study was designed to determine if overweight asthma patients would adhere to an alternate day calorie restriction (ADCR) dietary regimen, and to establish the effects of the diet on their symptoms, pulmonary function and markers of oxidative stress, and inflammation. Ten subjects with BMI > 30 were maintained for 8 weeks on a dietary regimen in which they ate ad libitum every other day, while consuming less than 20% of their normal calorie intake on the intervening days. At baseline, and at designated time points during the 8-week study, asthma control, symptoms, and Quality of Life questionnaires (ACQ, ASUI, mini-AQLQ) were assessed and blood was collected for analyses of markers of general health, oxidative stress, and inflammation.

Time-Restricted Feeding without Reducing Caloric Intake Prevents Metabolic Diseases in Mice Fed a High-Fat Diet

> ≡ http://www.sciencedirect.com/science/article/pii/S155041311200 1891

Two groups of mice consumed equivalent calories from a high fat diet. However, one group ate at their leisure while the other group ate on a time-restricted feeding schedule. The group fed on a time-restricted schedule experienced a protection from obesity, hyperinsulinemia, hepatic steatosis, inflammation and have improved motor coordination.

Improvements in LDL particle size and distribution by short-term alternate day modified fasting in obese adults

> ≡ https://www.cambridge.org/core/journals/british-journal-of-nutrition/article/improvements-in-ldl-particle-size-and-distribution-by-shortterm-alternate-day-modified-fasting-in-obese-adults/A11924C43D0E2B2F733935EB25D95DCD

These findings suggest that ADMF is an effective diet strategy for increasing LDL particle size and decreasing the proportion of small, dense LDL particles in obese adults.

Dose effects of modified alternate-day fasting regimens on in vivo cell proliferation and plasma insulin-like growth factor-1 in mice.

> ≡ http://www.ncbi.nlm.nih.gov/pubmed/17495119

Calorie restriction and cancer prevention: metabolic and molecular mechanisms

https://www.ncbi.nlm.nih.gov/pmc/articles/PMC2829867/

Fasting cycles retard growth of tumors and sensitize a range of cancer cell types to chemotherapy.

https://www.ncbi.nlm.nih.gov/pubmed/22323820

"These studies suggest that multiple cycles of fasting promote differential stress sensitization in a wide range of tumors and could potentially replace or augment the efficacy of certain chemotherapy drugs in the treatment of various cancers."

Improvement in coronary heart disease risk factors during an intermittent fasting/calorie restriction regimen: Relationship to adipokine modulations

https://www.ncbi.nlm.nih.gov/pmc/articles/PMC3514278/

Although both of the interventions produced favorable changes in lipids, superior modulations were shown in the IFCR-L group when compared to the IFCR-F group. The reductions in plasma lipids by IFCR-L (LDL-cholesterol: 19 percent, triglycerides: 20 percent) are similar to what has been reported in previous trials of IF

Intermittent Fasting Modulation of the Diabetic Syndrome in Streptozotocin-Injected Rats

https://www.hindawi.com/journals/ije/2012/962012/

Over 30 days, groups of 5-6 control or STZ rats were allowed free food access, starved overnight, or exposed to a restricted food supply comparable to that ingested by the intermittently fasting animals. Intermittent fasting improved glucose tolerance, increased plasma insulin, and lowered Homeostatis Model Assessment index. Caloric restriction failed to cause such beneficial effects.

Effects of short-term dietary restriction on survival of mammary ascites tumor-bearing rats.

> 🖹   https://www.ncbi.nlm.nih.gov/pubmed/3245934

The survival of tumor-bearing rats was enhanced by short-term relatively mild dietary restrictions.

> 🖹   https://www.ncbi.nlm.nih.gov/pmc/articles/PMC2815756/

Starvation-dependent differential stress resistance protects normal but not cancer cells against high-dose chemotherapy

> 🖹   https://www.ncbi.nlm.nih.gov/pmc/articles/PMC2448817/

Strategies to treat cancer have focused primarily on the killing of tumor cells. Here, we describe a differential stress resistance (DSR) method that focuses instead on protecting the organism but not cancer cells against chemotherapy. Short-term starved S. cerevisiae or cells lacking proto-oncogene homologs were up to 1,000 times better protected against oxidative stress or chemotherapy drugs than cells expressing the oncogene homolog Ras2val19. Low-glucose or low-serum media also protected primary glial cells but not six different rat and human glioma and neuroblastoma cancer cell lines against hydrogen peroxide or the chemotherapy drug/pro-oxidant cyclophosphamide. Finally, short-term starvation provided complete protection to mice but not to injected neuroblastoma cells against a high dose of the chemotherapy drug/pro-oxidant etoposide. These studies describe a starvation-based DSR strategy to enhance the efficacy of chemotherapy and suggest that specific agents among those that promote oxidative stress and DNA damage have the potential to maximize the differential toxicity to normal and cancer cells.

The Effects of Intermittent Energy Restriction on Indices of Cardiometabolic Health

http://ibimapublishing.com/articles/ENDO/2014/459119/

Current evidence from studies in rodents and humans demonstrates that IER (50-100percent ER on restricted days) is capable of promoting weight-loss and/or favorably cinfluencing an array of cardiometabolic health indices, with equal or greater efficacy than CER. In rodents, this has been shown to translate into improvements in clinical end-points such as disease progression. Putative mechanisms include the effects of IER on adipose physiology, stress resistance and acute ER-induced mobilization of fat distributed within visceral and intra-hepatic sites.

Caloric restriction and Intermittent Fasting: Two potential diets for successful brain aging

https://www.ncbi.nlm.nih.gov/pmc/articles/PMC2622429/

Consistent with the notion that stress resistance is highly coupled with life-span extension, activation of FoxO transcription factors in worms and flies increases longevity. FoxO proteins translate environmental stimuli, including the stress induced by caloric restriction into changes in gene expression programs that may coordinate organismal healthy aging and eventual longevity.

Usefulness of Routine Periodic Fasting to Lower Risk of Coronary Artery Disease among Patients Undergoing Coronary Angiography

https://www.ncbi.nlm.nih.gov/pmc/articles/PMC2572991/

Impact of intermittent fasting on health and disease processes.

https://www.ncbi.nlm.nih.gov/pubmed/27810402

Intermittent fasting (IF) encompasses eating patterns in which individuals go extended time periods (e.g., 16-48h) with little or no energy intake, with intervening periods of normal food intake, on a recurring basis. We use the term periodic fasting (PF) to refer to IF with periods of fasting or fasting mimicking diets lasting from two to as many as twenty- one or more days. In laboratory rats and mice IF and PF have profound beneficial effects on many different indices of health and, importantly, can counteract disease processes and improve functional outcome in experimental models of a wide range of age-related disorders including diabetes, cardiovascular disease, cancers and neurological disorders such as Alzheimer's disease Parkinson's disease and stroke. Studies of IF (e.g., 60 percent energy restriction on two days a week or every other day), PF (e.g., a five-day diet providing 750-1100kcal) and time-restricted feeding (TRF; limiting the daily period of food intake to eight hours or less) in normal and overweight human subjects have demonstrated efficacy for weight loss and improvements in multiple health indicators including insulin resistance and reductions in risk factors for cardiovascular disease.

Energy Intake and Exercise as Determinants of Brain Health and Vulnerability to Injury and Disease

https://www.ncbi.nlm.nih.gov/pmc/articles/PMC3518570/

Evolution favored individuals with superior cognitive and physical abilities under conditions of limited food sources, and brain function can therefore be optimized by intermittent dietary energy restriction (ER) and exercise. Such energetic challenges engage adaptive cellular stress response signaling pathways in neurons involving neurotrophic factors, protein chaperones, DNA repair proteins, autophagy and mitochondrial biogenesis. By suppressing adaptive cellular stress responses, overeating and a sedentary lifestyle may increase the risk of Alzheimer's and Parkinson's diseases, stroke, and depression. Intense concerted efforts of governments, families, schools and physicians will be required to successfully implement brain-healthy lifestyles that incorporate ER and exercise.

In conclusion, there is considerable evidence that intermittent ER and exercise during adult life will reduce the risk of deficits in brain function and neurodegenerative disorders. The cellular and molecular mechanisms by which energy intake and exercise affect neuroplasticity and vulnerability to disease have been partially established and involve either stimulation (IER and exercise) or suppression (overeating and lack of exercise) of adaptive cellular stress response signaling pathways. Optimal brain health may only be achieved by codifying and implementing prescriptions based upon energetic challenges.

Safety of alternate day fasting and effect on disordered eating behaviors

🗐 https://www.ncbi.nlm.nih.gov/pmc/articles/PMC4424827/

ADF produces minimal adverse outcomes, and has either benign or beneficial effects on eating disorder symptoms.

Diet restriction in rhesus monkeys lowers fasting and glucose-stimulated glucoregulatory end points.

https://www.ncbi.nlm.nih.gov/pubmed/7762649

Several measures of the insulin response (baseline, maximum, and integrated areas under curve) increased with age and were lower in DR monkeys. With the exception of glycated hemoglobin, which was not different in monkeys subjected to DR, these findings confirm previous studies in rodents demonstrating that DR alters glucose metabolism and may be related to the antiaging action of this intervention.

Role of Intermittent Fasting on Improving Health and Reducing Diseases

https://www.ncbi.nlm.nih.gov/pmc/articles/PMC4257368/

Effects of Intermittent Fasting on Metabolism in Men

http://www.sciencedirect.com/science/article/pii/S010442301300 0213

The development of cardiovascular disease, the leading cause of death worldwide, is directly connected to lifestyle factors causing metabolic disorders. Traditional approaches to counter these risk factors have been proven ineffective in most individuals. However, IF has recently been shown to have a positive impact on cardiovascular health.

Prolonged Fasting Reduces IGF-1/PKA to Promote Hematopoietic-Stem-Cell-Based Regeneration and Reverse Immunosuppression

http://www.cell.com/cell-stem-cell/fulltext/S1934-5909(16)00019-9

Saying No to Drugs: Fasting Protects Hematopoietic Stem Cells from Chemotherapy and Aging

> ✉ http://www.cell.com/cell-stem-cell/fulltext/S1934-5909(14)00203-3

Exercise and Fasting

Fasted Training? Exercise with low glycogen to be a better fuel burner

> ✉ http://conditioningresearch.blogspot.com/2012/10/fasted-training-exercise-with-low.html

8x Increase in "Mitochondria Building" Protein PGC1-Alpha W/ Medium Intensity Exercise in Glycogen Depleted Elite(!) Cyclists

> ✉ http://suppversity.blogspot.co.at/2012/10/8x-increase-in-mitochondria-building.html

Exercise with low glycogen increases PGC-1α gene expression in human skeletal muscle.

> ✉ http://www.ncbi.nlm.nih.gov/pubmed/23053125

Is Intermittent Fasting the magic pill for weight loss and muscle building, or just another fad?

Very good article about intermittent fasting particularly for those who wish to build muscle and might be concerned about possible muscle loss with intermittent fasting.

> ✉ http://www.muscleforlife.com/the-definitive-guide-to-intermittent-fasting/

A double-blind, placebo-controlled test of 2 d of calorie deprivation: effects on cognition, activity, sleep, and interstitial glucose concentrations.

📧 http://www.ncbi.nlm.nih.gov/pubmed/18779282

Dr. Michael Mosley (The Fast Diet)

Michael Mosley gained fame in the BBC documentary *Eat Fast Live Longer* where he not only interviews several experts on intermittent fasting but also becomes a human guinea pig and takes part in a fast himself. Following the success of the documentary he co-authored *The Fast Diet*, which is an Amazon best seller and discusses the specifics of intermittent fasting.

Interview with Dr. Michael Mosley, Author of *The Fast Diet*

📧 http://abcnews.go.com/GMA/video/fast-diet-creator-discusses-controversial-methods-gma-18763080

The hottest new trend in modern day weight loss

📧 http://abcnews.go.com/Health/feast-famine-controversial-fast-diet-weight-loss-plan/story?id=18613821

Eat Fast and Live Longer: Documentary Film

📧 http://www.dailymotion.com/video/xvdbtt_eat-fast-live-longer-hd_shortfilms

Mercola.Com

Dr. Joseph M. Mercola is an alternative medicine proponent, osteopathic physician. Mercola.com is one of the most well respected and most popular Natural Health Websites. A 1982 graduate of the Chicago College of Osteopathic Medicine he is a member of the

Association of American Physicians and Surgeons as well as several alternative medicine organizations and the author of two New York Times best sellers.

What the Science Says about Intermittent Fasting

> ✉ http://fitness.mercola.com/sites/fitness/archive/2013/06/28/intermittent-fasting-health-benefits.aspx

How Intermittent Fasting Stacks Up Among Obesity-Related Myths, Assumptions, and Evidence-Backed Facts

> ✉ http://fitness.mercola.com/sites/fitness/archive/2013/03/01/daily-intermittent-fasting.aspx

Intermittent Fasting Beats Traditional Diets and Even Chronic Calorie Restriction for Weight Loss and Other Health Benefits

> ✉ http://fitness.mercola.com/sites/fitness/archive/2013/12/20/intermittent-fasting-weight-loss.aspx

High-Intensity Interval Training and Intermittent Fasting - A Winning Combo for Fat Reduction and Optimal Fitness

> ✉ http://fitness.mercola.com/sites/fitness/archive/2012/11/02/interval-training-and-intermittent-fasting.aspx

Malnourishment and Mineral Deficiency in an Obese Society

This phenomenon has been widely documented. Below are some brief excerpts and links for further research.

Nutrient inadequacy in obese and non-obese youth

In this study, the Dietary Reference Intake standards were used to evaluate the prevalence of inadequate intakes of micronutrients in obese and non-obese youth.

> http://www.ncbi.nlm.nih.gov/pubmed/16332298

Homeless and Overweight: Obesity Is the New Malnutrition, Wired Magazine

The findings are the latest and most dramatic illustration of what's called the "hunger-obesity paradox," a term coined in 2005 by neurophysiologist Lawrence Scheier to describe the simultaneous presence of hunger and obesity.

> http://www.wired.com/wiredscience/2012/06/homeless-obesity/

Poorly nourished individuals can be seen at both ends of the spectrum (i.e., underweight AND overweight).

> http://www.myfooddiary.com/resources/ask_the_expert/overweight_malnourished.asp

Mineral deficiency is common in America today - are you mineral deficient?

According to the USDA, in 1953 a person could get all the vitamin A he or she needed from eating two peaches. Today, you would have to eat 50 peaches! The depletion of minerals from our soils has resulted from over farming, overuse of pesticides, herbicides, and fertilizers. Fruits, vegetables, and grains grown in these soils are mineral deficient. Therefore, we can no longer get sufficient minerals from our food to supply our body's needs.

> http://www.examiner.com/article/mineral-deficiency-is-common-america-today-are-you-mineral-deficient

Dietary Magnesium and C-reactive Protein Levels

According to a study sponsored by the National Institutes of Health shows that 68 percent of Americans are deficient in magnesium. Most Americans consume magnesium at levels below the RDA. Individuals with intakes below the RDA are more likely to have elevated CRP, which may contribute to cardiovascular disease risk.

> ≡ http://www.mccordresearch.com/sites/default/files/research/diet
> ary_magnesium_and_c_reactive_protein.pdf

78879867R00093

Made in the USA
San Bernardino, CA
09 June 2018